The True Faith and How I Found It

THE STORY OF A REMARKABLE CONVERSION FROM ROMAN CATHOLICISM, WITH ADDITIONAL CHAPTERS ON SUBJECTS VITAL AND FUNDAMENTAL

BY
Rev. SAMUEL McGERALD, D. D.

[All Rights Reserved]

1912
TRUE FAITH COMPANY
NEW YORK and BUFFALO, N. Y.
ISBN 1-4196-7610-5

"Contend earnestly for the faith which was *once for all* delivered unto the Saints."—(REV. VERS.)

—*Jude*.

CONTENTS

Chapter.		Page.
I.	My Early Years.	11
II.	Boyhood Experiences	17
III.	Coming to America	21
IV.	A Turning Point in My Life	25
V.	Reading the Sealed Book	29
VI.	The Word Winning Its Way	34
VII.	Worship of the Virgin.	39
VIII.	At a Protestant Church	44
IX.	The Gibraltar of the Papacy	48
X.	Transubstantiation	52
XI.	The Sacrifice of the Mass.	59
XII.	Reaching a Crisis.	65
XIII.	The Darkness Before Dawn.	71
XIV.	The Morning Breaks.	76
XV.	Tried as by Fire	81
XVI.	Mother Hull in Evidence	88
XVII.	A Priest at a Methodist Class Meeting	93
XVIII.	Calling at a Convent.	98

CONTENTS—*Continued*

Chapter.		Page.
XIX.	The Profits of Purgatory	102
XX.	The New Life	107
XXI.	The Immaculate Conception	111
XXII.	The Papacy and the Murder of Heretics	121
XXIII.	Rome and Sin	130
XXIV.	The Forgiveness of Sin	134
XXV.	Rome and the Bible	139
XXVI.	Rome and Indulgences	145
XXVII.	The Central Doctrine of Rome Overthrown	149
XXVIII.	Half Communion	152
XXIX.	A Striking Parallel	156
XXX.	Priestly Rule Unfavorable	158
XXXI.	A Damaging Dogma	161
XXXII.	Peter and the Rock	164

FOREWORD

WHILE the Rev. Dr. William Butler, who founded the mission of the Methodist Episcopal Church in India, was under appointment to establish a mission in Mexico, he visited, before going, many of the churches throughout the country, presenting the cause and awakening an interest in the work. The first church he visited was that at Benton Centre, Yates County, N. Y., of which I was then pastor. A large and enthusiastic meeting was held in the church, and a generous contribution was given in aid of the new mission.

The next morning, at the breakfast table, Dr. Butler drew from me a relation of the story of my conversion from Roman Catholicism to Bible Christianity. He became deeply interested in the narrative and urged me very strongly to write it out for him for publication, which I then promised to do. I made a beginning, but did not finish it. Since then many have spoken to me about committing it to writing, among whom are some of our leading ministers. During the more than fifty years since I became a minister of the Gospel I have been invited hundreds of times to tell in various churches the story of the great change in my life. Many Roman Catholics have come to hear me, and as I have avoided the use of all terms or expressions that might be offensive they have always given me an attentive hearing.

Witnessing on such occasions the interest awakened among both Protestants and Catholics the conviction invariably has been revived that I ought to put the story in permanent form, but other pressing duties have deterred me from undertaking the task.

In bringing out the present edition I have revised, and enlarged somewhat, the original book entitled "From Rome to Protestantism," and added several very important chapters which will greatly enhance its value.

The new title, "The True Faith and How I Found It," is more in accord with the spirit of the story than the former. For the quest was not for an "ism," or even a church, but for "the truth as it is in Jesus." I was well grounded in the faith of the old historic Church, but through the reading of the Gospels and the writings of the Apostles my mind was awakened and quickened into a new life. *I began to think.* Then I found that the mutterings of a man in a dead tongue brought no sense of forgiveness of sin; prayers to dead saints, or the Virgin Mary, left no asssurance of answers thereto; and a wafer blessed by a priest was a poor substitute for Him who says, "I AM THE BREAD OF LIFE."

I therefore instinctively sought Him of whom the Apostle Peter declared: "Thou art the Christ, the Son of the living God." Feeling as the Philippian jailor did when "trembling for fear, he fell down before Paul and Silas and said, 'Sirs, what must I do to be saved?'" I received with joy the welcome response: "Believe on the Lord Jesus, and thou shalt be saved." There and then I found a sure resting place. The promise of Jesus was verified unto me: "Come unto Me, and I will give you rest;" and "He that believeth on the Son hath eternal life." This belief or faith that saves, and which I sought and found, is not faith in a man, or creed, or church, but in the divine Person, the Son of God.

"Faith of our Fathers! holy faith! We will be true to thee till death!"

I.

MY EARLY YEARS

MY Birthplace was Glenavy, **County Antrim**, Ireland, eleven miles from Belfast.

My father was a well-to-do farmer, having three or four tenant houses on his place. He was also what was there called a " linen draper," taking the linen yarn from the manufacturers of Belfast and Lisburn, and giving it out to be woven by his tenants and others in the neighbourhood. He had three or four looms in his own house which he kept in constant operation. He also kept a small country store. On account of his strict integrity and generous disposition he was held in very high esteem by all who knew him. His neighbours gave him the familiar sobriquet, " honest John," of which epithet his children were never ashamed. Unfortunately he went security to a large amount for a brother-in-law, a business man of reputed means, who afterwards failed in business, leaving my father to pay the whole amount, which crippled his affairs so seriously that he was led eventually to sell out and emigrate to America. He would not, however, have done so had it not been for his large family of children. He knew it would be better for them.

My father was a devout and zealous Roman Catholic, and to the best of his ability trained his children in that faith. I never knew him to use a profane word, nor would he allow his boys to use even by-words. When Father Matthew, the " apostle of temperance," passed through our part of the country, my father took the pledge from his hand and kept it inviolate to the day of his death. In view of the example he should set before his family, he was persuaded by my mother to take this important step, and she, in order to encourage him, accompanied him to the church and kneeling by his side at the chancel took the pledge with him. In proof of the deep impression this event made upon my young heart, I would say that the greatest care that burdened my mind during those early years was the fear that father might fall into temptation and break his pledge. I thought that if he should do that he would lose his soul.

My father was accustomed to do what I have never known or heard of a Catholic family doing in America; he had family prayers during the seasons of Lent and Advent. Every night during those periods the family was brought together, and the Rosary of the Blessed Virgin Mary was recited. The Rosary is the most popular and interesting of all the religious forms of prayer prescribed by the Church. It is beautifully arranged, and when entered into with devout intention and read reverently is a very impressive service. It is designed to be a sort of abridgment of the Gospel, a history of the life, sufferings, and triumphant victory of Jesus Christ. Aside from certain brief meditations on certain phases of the life of Christ, it is composed of three prayers; namely, the Lord's Prayer, the Hail Mary, and the Doxology. It is divided into five parts; each part closing with the Lord's Prayer, once; and the Hail Mary, *ten times*. So that during the service of the Rosary the devout Roman Catholic prays to the

MY EARLY YEARS.   13

Lord five times, and to the Virgin Mary *fifty times.* This is the prayer offered to her : " Holy Mary, Mother of God, pray for us sinners, now and at the hour of our death, Amen."

In repeating the Rosary, the devout Roman Catholic generally makes use of the beads. The string of beads used has been blessed by the priest. It is divided into five sections. Each division has ten small beads and at the end a large bead, which are used to keep tally during the service. The supplicant holds the string in his hand, and on the offering of a Hail Mary, drops one of the small beads, and so continues until the ten have been recited, and when the large bead is reached, the Lord's Prayer is offered, and so on until the circle is completed.

My mother's maiden name was Young. She was brought up a Protestant, I believe a Presbyterian, though concerning her early religious history I have never been able to learn much. I never knew definitely all the circumstances which led to the change, but as near as I have been able to learn it was in this wise : My mother's father was dead, and her mother was left with a large number of children. The eldest son, Samuel, was in school. I have always supposed it was a Catholic school. At all events, while there, through certain influences brought to bear upon him, he became a Roman Catholic, and in the flush of his new born life and zeal went home, and was the means of turning the entire family—all except the eldest daughter, who had married and emigrated to America shortly before this. The young man, Samuel, then studied for the priesthood, and became one of the most distinguished priests of his day in those parts. My mother was a bright, intelligent woman, and owing to this change of doctrinal views, became deeply interested in the controversy between Roman Catholics and Protestants. She read extensively on her side of the question, had a good memory and a good command of language, and was favoured with an attractive address and a winning disposition, which gave her great influence among her acquaintances and friends. And as her family was the only branch that separated from the faith of its fathers, she had many an opportunity of defending her position, as she came in contact with her friends and relatives. Therefore, the differences between the two faiths and the arguments and proofs in favour of the one and against the other were subject of well-nigh daily conversation in the family ; all of which made a profound impression upon my young mind.

I was baptized by my uncle, the Rev. Samuel Young, who gave me his name, and designed educating me for the priesthood. According to the teaching of the Church when I was baptized I was born again. The sacrament of baptism, when duly and properly administered by either priest, layman, or even heretic, washes away original sin, in which we are at first born ; remits all actual sins, which we ourselves have committed (in case we have committed any before baptism) both as to the guilt and pain ; infuses the habit of divine grace into the soul, and makes us the adopted children of God ; gives a right and title to the kingdom of heaven ; imprints a character or spiritual mark in the soul ; and, in fine, lets us into the Church of God, and makes us children and members of the Church. (Dr. Challoner's Catholic Christian Instructed.)

MY EARLY YEARS. 15

I do not remember when I made my first confession to the priest. I remember, however, when I received the sacrament of confirmation, and it must have been about that time that I first went to confession.

The Roman Catholic Church recognizes seven sacraments: Baptism, Confirmation, the Lord's Supper, Penance, Extreme Unction, Holy Orders, and Matrimony.

Confirmation is not usually given until a person is come to years of understanding. The sacrament is administered by the Bishop, who, turning towards those who are to be confirmed, with his hands joined before his breast, says, " May the Holy Ghost come down upon us, and the power of the Most High keep you from sins." Then extending his hands towards those who are to be confirmed he prays that they may receive the Holy Ghost. He then makes the sign of the cross with holy chrism, a compound of oil of olives and balm of Gilead, solemnly consecrated by the Bishop on Maunday-Thursday, the day before Good Friday : the anointing of the forehead is to represent the inward anointing of the Holy Ghost. The Bishop also gives a little blow on the cheek of the person that is confirmed to indicate that, like a true soldier of Jesus Christ, he is to suffer all kinds of affronts and injuries for his faith.

When thus confirmed, I was taught to believe that I received the seven-fold gift of the Holy Spirit, and was thus fortified against all visible and invisible enemies of the faith. I was not conscious, however, of any change having occurred. Surely if I had received such a wonderful blessing as the gift of the Holy Ghost I would have known it. But it was not my fault, nor the fault of the officiating Bishop, that no spiritual change **took place** in the administration of the rite. I had not the faith to open my heart to receive the Holy Spirit. And the Bishop's touch was powerless to produce the great change. I have never yet met a Roman Catholic who acknowledged that he had experienced a change of heart or had received any special gift or grace as the result of the interposition of either priest or prelate.

II.

BOYHOOD EXPERIENCES

OWING to my father's standing in the parish I was brought into close and very pleasant relations with the priests.

There had been four priests connected with the parish within my recollection whom I knew right well. The first was Father MacMullen. For a time he boarded with us, and I was a great favorite of his. He was evidently a good man, for he was noted throughout the parish for his piety, and when he died there was sincere lamentation over him. He was also regarded as a great preacher, and I distinctly recall the effects produced upon the people by his fervent and stirring appeals to lead a better life, and how they would weep and respond audibly during the sermon. This was something very unusual, and evidenced the influence he had over the people.

His successor, a jolly, genial, good-hearted man, was not, however, noted for his piety. He might have been, had it not been for his love of whiskey. Having to " serve mass " every morning, before going to school, I was at his home every day ; and many times in the week was I sent after school to the neighbouring tavern to have the black bottle filled. At one time while I was gone, a brother of the priest came from a distance to see him, so the servant girl intercepted me with the order from Father C—— not to bring the bottle into the house but to hide it in the barn, which I did. Although he had that personal failing, he exhorted his flock most eloquently to habits of temperance. And while Father Matthew was passing through those parts on his great teetotal crusade, Father C—— gave out from the altar that on a certain Sunday he would administer the Father Matthew pledge and wished everyone to take it, with the encouraging promise that he would set the good example himself. The announcement that the priest was going to take the pledge awakened the deepest interest throughout the parish, and made the hearts of all the people glad, for they knew no one needed to do so more than he. But, unfortunately, when the day arrived he failed to make good his promise, and though he did his best to get all his parishioners to sign the pledge, he placed himself under no obligations to abstain. In time he was removed by the Bishop, and it was understood afterward that he reformed.

I might say at this point that in case a Roman priest has inherited a taste for strong drink the temptation for him to indulge too freely and acquire the habit of intemperance is very strong. He is required to say mass every morning in the year, fasting. During its celebration the wine used, which is the very best brand, is drunk by the priest, the people being denied the cup. A small sip, a thimble-full would suffice, but generally the quantity used is a good-sized wine glass full. While serving mass I have poured it out of the little cruet into the chalice held by the priest hundreds of times, and he always held it until he got the last drop therefrom.

Father C—— was followed by Father Hanna, a devoted young priest and a good preacher. I have a very vivid recollection of a service held in the church on Good

BOYHOOD EXPERIENCES. 19

Friday, when during the sermon the priest, holding a crucifix in his hand, gave such a graphic description of the sufferings of Christ upon the cross for the sins of the world that he broke down in tears himself, being unable to proceed for a while, and a remarkable scene of weeping in the congregation followed.

Father Denver was the priest in charge of the parish when we emigrated to this country. He was very different from all his predecessors. He was temperate in his habits, but very stern, haughty, and over-bearing in his manners. He ruled his people with a rod of iron. He would occasionally horsewhip an incorrigible offender. And though the people nicknamed him "The Bull Dog" on account of his severity of discipline, yet he commanded their submission to his authority, and to a certain degree their respect. He and my uncle, the priest, were good friends, and it was arranged with my father and mother that these two priests were to retain and educate me for the priesthood. Arrangements were all made to that effect, but when the time came to make the final transfer, mother refused to give me up. Her excuse to them was that she could not part with me, but to the family she frankly said that she was afraid to leave me under their care, knowing the severity of both.

My uncle's parish adjoined the one in which we lived, and though he but seldom came to our house, I often met him at his mother's. Grandmother lived about four miles from us, was in good circumstances, and the neighbouring priests occasionally met there for a good time socially. On one of these occasions a number of priests came together on the invitation of my uncle. In the evening, after supper, they assembled in the parlor to drink wine and play cards. As I was a mere lad, and a special favorite of my uncle, bearing his name, I was admitted to the room and sat by the grate fire while the priests drank and played. But that in which I was most interested, and which made the deepest impression upon me, was the silver that lay upon the table and that changed hands during the evening. It did not occur to me that there was anything wrong in it. But later I understood that they were gambling. From the parlor and the priests I passed out into the kitchen, where I remember seeing the hired men engaged in the same business—drinking and gambling Like priest, like people. Such things, however, occasioned no remark.

III.

COMING TO AMERICA

WHEN my parents first decided to leave Ireland, they planned emigrating to Australia, and, indeed, my father had engaged passage for the family, and had paid a given sum down. But through the intervention of a friend of the family who had decided to go with us, father changed his mind and took passage for America. The interposition seemed providential, as the vessel on which we were to sail for Australia was lost on her out-bound voyage, and all on board perished four hundred passengers besides the crew.

When my parents first talked of emigrating to America it was their intention to go to Illinois, where my mother's eldest sister lived, the one who had left Ireland before the family became Roman Catholics. Her husband's name was McClure. They lived a hundred miles from Chicago, in the Rock River country. I remember the letters which we used to receive from them bore the postmark " Rock River Rapids," but there is no such post-office there now. They had a large family of children, and their eldest daughter married a man by the name of Dixon, who lived where the town of Dixon is now located.

It was supposed the arrangements were all completed for our removal to that part of America, and my Uncle McClure was to meet us at the village of Chicago with ox teams and convey us all to his home. But all at once the plans were changed, and another destination was fixed upon. Instead of sailing to New York it was decided we should take shipping for Quebec. Although but little was said concerning the change of plan, yet it was understood among us children that it was on account of my uncle's family being Protestants. It was feared that they might have an influence upon us. At all events the idea of locating upon a Western prairie was abandoned, and correspondence between the two families was entirely discontinued from that time. After this the names of my uncle and his family were never mentioned, and no effort was put forth after we arrived here to open correspondence with them. All of which appeared to us children as mysterious. Now I think I understand the reason for it all.

On the fourth of April, 1845, we bade adieu to the friends and scenes of our childhood's years. Arriving at Belfast, we sailed to Liverpool, where we tarried a week, waiting for the vessel to sail. After a stormy passage of forty-five days we landed in Quebec, and from thence came to Toronto, where we staid for a couple of months and then came on to Dundas, a town six miles west of the city of Hamilton. There we lived three years. During that time we occupied the Rectory. Father William O'Reilly was the priest, that being his first parish. He was a young man of great energy and force of character, a good man and a good preacher. He was highly respected by Protestants as well as by his own people. Living in the same house with us, mother preparing his meals and taking care of his rooms, and I waiting on him by " serving mass " every morning, I was thus brought into close relationship with him. I formed a very warm attachment for him, which I think was mutual, and even after my conversion to

COMING TO AMERICA.

Protestantism, on re-visiting Dundas, I always went to see him, when we had a good visit together.

During all this time I never came under any but Catholic influence. There were just two incidents of a religious nature that during those years made a lasting impression on my mind. The one was a sermon preached by Father O'Reilly. It was a long time after he entered upon his parish work before he commenced preaching. I remember very distinctly that after he had been there eleven weeks, and had not preached his first sermon, I asked my father why it was that Father O'Reilly did not preach. Father answered, " He is getting ready," But when he got ready and began to preach he gave some very earnest, excellent sermons. The incident I refer to which impressed me so deeply was this : I had been to confession on Sunday morning just before mass. I have no recollection of the nature of my confession or of the sins I recounted, but I remember as though it were yesterday when the priest came to preach his sermon it seemed as if every word were meant for me. He preached with great earnestness and power, and the truth searched me through and through, so that I remember trembling under its power. I was surely then convicted of sin.

The other incident occurred on a Sunday evening, when all the family were gone except two of my younger sisters and myself. Father had, as an heir-loom in the family, a very large illustrated edition of the Rheimish New Testament. It contained the family record, and was regarded as a very sacred treasure, and, therefore, was but seldom opened. But that night, while we were alone, I took it down and read from it to my sisters the story of the arrest, trial, and crucifixion of Jesus. The simple reading of the narrative made such an impression on us that we all broke down and wept together. I was in my thirteenth year, and I have no doubt that the spirit of the Lord wrought then upon my youthful heart.

Some of the men for, and with whom, I worked in Canada, were very bad men. There was drinking and gambling and profanity going on more or less every day and night without any counteracting good influences. I was compelled to go to the saloon to get beer for the men to drink, and had to listen to their obscene and vile language daily. Those men all nominally belonged to the Roman Catholic Church, but they were " bad Catholics," and were living contrary to the teachings of their Church. My father had always been very careful in bringing up his boys, and never would allow the use of any bad language. Even expressions that may be regarded as perfectly harmless he forbade the use of in the family. But my daily association with bad men and boys in the shop exerted a baneful influence upon my young life, an influence which home teaching and parental restraint did not fully counteract

IV.

A TURNING POINT IN MY LIFE

IN the fall of 1848, my father with his family moved from Dundas, Ontario, to Rochester, N.Y. I was then in my sixteenth year. Up to that time I had always been under Catholic influence. I had never been inside a Protestant Church nor had a Protestant ever spoken to me of my religious belief. I was now for the first time brought under other influences. My father had a large family, and all of us who were able were obliged to assist in its support. In looking for employment it was a long time before I could find anything to do, until finally I engaged with a man to drive a team on the Erie Canal. The time being appointed when I was to begin work my father accompanied me to the place where I was to meet my employer, but he failed to appear, and after waiting some time, I suggested that we try some other place. It so happened, in God's good providence, that the first place we entered I found employment. That was the turning-point in my life, the most important event that had occurred in my history. I have always regarded it as a special providence that at this juncture I should have been so highly favored.

My new employer was a very kind man. He was also an earnest, practical, every-day Christian. The moral atmosphere of my surroundings was pure, helpful, elevating. The contrast between this new environment and that where I had worked in Dundas was so marked that it seemed like heaven to me. This man was the first Protestant Christian with whom I had ever been brought in contact. James Henderson was a leading and honoured member of the First Methodist Episcopal Church of that city. Although reared in the Protestant faith, he was yet well informed in the doctrines and usages of the Roman Catholic Church, and took great delight, also, in conversing on the subject, and in debating the doctrinal differences of the two faiths.

It was not long after I entered his employ before he introduced the subject of religion to me, and I always held myself in readiness to give a prompt answer to his questions and to defend the faith of my Church. Though young, I was well versed in the Catechism and Challoner's "Catholic Christian Instructed." And, owing to my mother's change of faith in Ireland, and the controversies with her Protestant relatives thas followed, I had become well informed in regard to the points of difference between the two religions, and felt very confident that I could hold my own in an ordinary debate with a Protestant. The conversations that occurred from time to time between my employer and myself became deeply interesting, and at times quite exciting. I would go home and report the situation to my mother, who would encourage me in the good work and supply me with any needed argument or proof-text. There were times when the interest arising from these discussions was all-absorbing, and I would retire at night with my mind filled with the thoughts awakened thereby, dream about it, and arise in the morning with the subject uppermost in my mind.

I had not been long in the employ of Mr Henderson before I was impressed with the fact that he was a good

A TURNING POINT IN MY LIFE. 27

man, considerate, and apparently thoughtful of my temporal welfare. By degrees, without any apparent effort on his part, he won his way into my heart. He gave me a different idea than I ever had before of the character of Protestant Christians. He also seemed to take a special interest in me. He told me of a certain distinguished Irishman who had been brought up a Roman Catholic, but who had become a Protestant, and who had written a book that was then having a large sale. The name of the book was " Kirwan's letters to Bishop Hughes." The man who had addressed this series of letters to the Bishop over the pseudonym of " Kirwan " was the Rev. Nicholas Murray, D.D., of Elizabeth City, N.J. Mr Henderson wanted to know if I would read the book if he brought it to me. I told him certainly I would, I was not afraid of his book. But the reading of those letters did not make a favorable impression upon me at that time. The book contained the relation of many incidents which I regarded as exaggerations, if not fabrications. The writer told of certain things that he had seen in the South of Ireland, and as I came from the North and Roman Catholicism differs materially in the two sections of the country, in its discipline and usages, I cast the book one side and pronounced it a pack of lies.

He then told me of another great Irishman, Dr. Adam Clark, who spent over thirty years in writing a commentary on the Bible, and he wanted to know if I would read his comments. I said, " Yes, bring them on." He did so, and directed my attention to those passages in the New Testament where the author touches on controversial points, such as Matt. 26, and John 6. The style and the matter were so different from "Kirwan" that I became deeply interested in his writings, and received considerable light from reading his various comments. He was very clear, thorough, and rational in his treatment of all those passages pertaining to the doctrine of transubstantiation; and there was a deep spiritual tone to his writings that attracted and held my attention. "Kirwan" I had no use for. He threw no light upon the Scriptures. What he said about and against the Catholic Church might have been ever so true, but instead of convincing me it awakened feelings of resentment and indignation. It was different with Clark. He was convincing, scriptural, reverent, and fair, at least so I thought, and I was favorably impressed by him.

V.

READING THE SEALED BOOK

ALTHOUGH I became quite interested in reading certain portions of Clark's Commentary, yet I found nothing that quite suited my case. There was an instinctive craving, though I could not then interpret it, for something deeper and diviner than the words of man.

It was in September I went to work for my new employer. In the progress of the daily conversations we had on the subject of religion our interest in each other seemed to increase, and the desire to aid each other was mutual. While he was endeavouring in every possible way to interest me in the reading of the Bible, I was equally interested and zealous in trying to convince him of the error of his ways and lead him into the true fold. His noble, sympathetic nature, and the intensely practical and common-sense character of his religion won my confidence. I had no doubt of his sincerity, but that would not save him. As there was no salvation out of the true Church it became my duty to do my utmost to win his soul. Finally the hope sprang up in my heart that I might be the means of his salvation. Consequently I went home and told mother of my self-appointed mission. She saw my faith and zeal, and instead of checking me in my ardent hopes she encouraged me in my first effort to propagate the faith, and did all in her power from time to time to help me in my bold undertaking.

As I thought the matter over, however, I saw that I must be able to meet him on his own ground. By this time I had discovered that he had no special reverence for my Catechism. He would not accept the statements that it contained in lieu of Holy Scripture. I was at first surprised at that, as I had been taught from infancy that the Catechism took the precedence of the Bible. The Bible could be understood by the laity only as explained or interpreted by the Church, and the Catechism is that interpretation. And, therefore, it is practically of higher authority, and should be read and observed by the laity in preference to the Scriptures. But as my friend whom I was trying to convert would not accept the Catechism in proof of the doctrines and the faith I held, I saw I must bring forth Scripture proof to offset his arguments. To do that I must read the Bible. *That was the motive that led me to read it.* The book lay on the bench. I did not stop to inquire which version it was, whether " Douay " or " King James." It was the first copy of the Bible I had ever seen. Up to this time I had not ventured to open it to read it. But now my desire was so strong to confute the errors of this good but misguided man and win him to the true faith, I began to read the wonderful book.

Had I been as well informed then as I was afterward in regard to the teaching of the Church in reference to the reading of the Bible, especially the Protestant version, I would not have ventured on such a hazardous experiment.

Notwithstanding the fact that there have been issued from time to time authoritative decrees by popes and councils against the indiscriminate reading of the Scrip-

READING THE SEALED BOOK. 31

tures, yet there is great diversity of opinion among members of the Church of Rome respecting this subject. Some are for the promiscuous reading of them, some are not. Some would give them without note or comment others would not. Thus we perceive great variety of sentiment exists among Catholics ; but in general they either entirely discountenance the reading of Scripture by the laity, or they so limit its exercise as to come nearly to an entire prohibition. While I had been counselled by my priests not to read the Bible, having been told by them that it was a dangerous book for the laity to read, I never yet heard a priest in public or private advise the reading even of the Catholic version, with notes and comments. Time and again have the priests quoted to me Peter's words in regard to Paul, where he says : " Even as our beloved brother Paul according to the wisdom given unto him hath written ; as also in all his epistles, speaking in them of these things, in which are some hard to be understood, which they that are unlearned and unstable wrest, as they do also the other Scriptures, unto their own destruction." They never, however, would quote what Peter says in the following sentence : " but grow in the knowledge of our Lord and Saviour Jesus Christ." And in another place Peter tells us how we are to grow : " As new-born babes, desire the *sincere milk of the word*, that ye may grow thereby." This same apostle, whom the Church of Rome claims was the first pope, teaches plainly that the new birth, which Jesus says we must experience before we can enter the kingdom of God, is the result of the implanting of the incorruptible seed, *the Word of God*, which liveth and abideth forever. But how can the word be in our hearts for the Spirit to act upon unless we read it or hear it ? And Paul commends Timothy that from a child he had known the Holy Scriptures, which were able to make him wise unto salvation.

Moved by the pious motive to do good, and led by the Spirit of Truth Himself, I opened the old Book for light. I was strong in the faith. My religious yearnings were intense. I longed to do good. I was very strict in the observance of all the rules of the Church. On the recurrence of the special festivals of the Church I was always the first in the family to suggest their observance and to lead the way to the confessional.

I cannot now recall the exact time when I began the reading of the Sacred Volume. It was late in the fall. I remember, however, as though it were but yesterday, the first impressions made upon my mind. I opened it to find proof-texts to convince my opponent and secure his conversion. I had entered upon a greater task than I had bargained for. Ere I was aware I was charmed with the book. It held me, as it were, spellbound. I became deeply interested in the stories of the Old Testament, especially those of Abraham and Joseph and Daniel. My interest in reading it became so intense that I would sit up till midnight poring over its pages. I became an enthusiastic student. I had found a hidden treasure and I must needs tell of it. The joy was too great to conceal, so on Sunday when I went home, as all the children were wont to, I would tell them of the Old Book. I tried to tell them of some of the wonderful things I had found in it. I deemed it a wonderful discovery. In the simplicity of my heart and the fervor of my newborn zeal, I ventured one Sunday afternoon

READING THE SEALED BOOK.

to take the book home with me that I might read to an older brother some of those striking passages I had found. As I became so deeply interested in the reading of the book, my people began to talk about it, and though they never mistrusted that there was any danger of my views on religion undergoing any change, they would occasionally make some playful remark concerning my new departure in reading. One day, mother remarked: "What a Bible reader Samuel is becoming! It may be that some day he may become a Methodist preacher!" which was the last thought that anyone of us seriously entertained.

VI.

THE WORD WINNING ITS WAY

"THE entrance of Thy word giveth Light." The truth of that Scripture was verified in my experience. The first effect of the reading of the Word of which I was conscious was that it set me thinking; it awakened inquiry; it proved to be living and powerful and sharper than any two-edged sword, and was a discerner of the thoughts and intents of the heart. I could say with the Psalmist, "Thy testimonies are wonderful." I could not give the day or date when the light began to dawn on my mind. It was like the breaking of the day, silent, imperceptible, but none the less real. The reading of the Word of God was to me a revelation, opening up a new world. In searching for proof-texts to confute and win my opponent and friend, I found the pearl of truth. I received new views of God's love and mercy, and of Jesus' compassion and power.

Of the few passages of Scripture that had been drilled into my mind from infancy was Peter's remark about certain things in Paul's writings that were hard to be understood, and therefore the best way was for the laity to let the Bible alone. But as I read I found so much of it that was comforting, helpful, and inspiring, that I devoured it as a hungry man would devour nutritious food. I not only found the hidden treasure, but the Word found me.

As I read the Old Testament, I was impressed with the fact that the good men there mentioned offered prayer direct to God, without the mediation of saint or angel. And in the New Testament I saw no evidence of the intervention of the Mother of Jesus between His disciples and Himself. They either approached Jesus directly or they came to the Father in the name of Jesus. And there is not an iota of evidence between the lids of the Bible of any advocate or mediator coming between the soul and its Redeemer. This made a profound impression upon my mind. Indeed it was at this point that the foundation of my old faith began to give way to doubt, and the more I read and thought and prayed, the more unsettled I became in my views in regard to the worship of the Virgin Mary, until at last I was compelled by the force of my convictions to give up the " Hail Mary," the " Rosary of the Blessed Virgin," and the " Litany of the Saints," and simply offer up the Lord's Prayer, or pray to the Father in the name of Jesus.

The reason my mind was first directed to this error of the Roman Church arose from the fact that I became bewildered and perplexed in mind as I prayed to Mary and the Saints. I never had any satisfaction in going through the " Litany of the Saints " or the " Rosary of the Virgin." That Sts. Peter, or Paul, or Patrick, or Mary or Bridget; or any holy virgin, saint or martyr should be able to hear and answer so many suppliants all at once appeared to me to be beyond reason or common sense, as it was contrary to Holy Scripture. The more I read the more clearly convinced I became.

As I read the Gospels I was greatly surprised to find that Jesus, while treating His Mother with the greatest respect, yet never called her " mother," but always addressed her as " Woman." When at the marriage in

Cana of Galilee, St. John says, "the mother of Jesus was there. And when they wanted wine, the mother of Jesus saith unto him, 'They have no wine.' Jesus saith unto her, 'Woman, what have I to do with thee? Mine hour is not yet come.'" St. Matthew, in his Gospel, relates this remarkable incident whic. certainly furnishes no evidence or proof of divine authority for the worship of Mary, which is now becoming the distinctive worship of the Roman Catholic Church : "While he yet talked to the people, his mother and his brethren stood without, desiring to speak with him. Then one said unto him, 'Behold, thy mother and thy brethren stand without, desiring to speak with thee.' But he answered and said unto him, 'Who is my mother? and who are my brethren?' And he stretched forth his hand toward his disciples and said, 'Behold my mother and my brethren! For whosoever shall do the will of my Father which is in heaven, the same is my brother, and sister, and mother.'" Matthew 12 : 46-50.

How foreign to the worship of the Virgin is such an incident as that! At another time as he was talking to the people, a certain woman of the company lifted up her voice, and said unto Jesus, "Blessed is the womb that bare thee, and the paps which thou hast sucked." But Jesus at once replied, "Yea rather, blessed are they that hear the word of God, and keep it." Luke 11 : 27-28. Thus our Lord, knowing all things and anticipating the worship that one day would be given his mother, guards every utterance that might be construed as favoring an undue reverence that might be rendered her. Further, take the last time that she is mentioned in the Gospels. The statement is found in John 19 :

26-27. "As Jesus hung on the cross he saw his mother, and the disciple standing by whom he loved (John), he said unto his mother, 'Woman, behold thy son!' Then said he to the disciple, 'Behold thy mother!' And from that hour that disciple took her unto his own home."

In my Bible reading I left the Gospels and searched the other books of the New Testament, and to my utter surprise, I never found her name mentioned after the 14th verse of the first chapter of the Acts. Surely, I thought, John, the beloved disciple, who took the mother of Jesus home with him from the cross, and with whom she spent the rest of her days, will have something to say about praying to her in the letters he wrote, in his Gospel, in the Revelation. But he never mentions her name. So, likewise, with Peter, whom Catholics claim was the first Pope, there is not a word in all his writings in regard to this phase of present-day worship in the Roman Church. I turned to a letter that the Apostle Paul wrote to the Church at Rome, and even in that her name is never mentioned. But on the other hand, I found certain passages of Scripture which were positively against the intercession of Mary or any saint or angel; passages which inculcate and emphasize the advocacy of the Lord Jesus Christ. 1 John 2: 1—"If any man sin, we have an advocate with the Father, Jesus Christ the righteous." 1 Tim. 2: 5—"There is one God and one mediator between God and men, the Man Jesus Christ." Acts 4: 12—"There is none other name under heaven given among men, whereby we must be saved."

What should I do? Give heed to the conflicting

views of fallible men in regard to the worship of creatures ? or hearken to the voice of God, saying, "Thou shalt worship the Lord thy God, and him only shalt thou serve ? "

I knew the distinctions which the Roman Catholic Church makes respecting the matter of worship. Of sacred or religious adoration there are three kinds, viz., *latria*, *hyperdulia*, and *dulia*. Adoration, or the worship of *latria*, is that which is due to God alone. The adoration or worship of *hyperdulia* is that which is due and rendered to the Blessed Virgin on account of her being, as they claim, the Mother of God. The worship of *dulia* is that which is given to the saints and angels. Now, the truth is, there is not one Catholic in a million who stops to distinguish between these different kinds of worship. Nor can he. What do the masses of ignorant worshippers know concerning such nice distinctions expressed in a dead language ?

Attributes belonging to God alone are ascribed to Mary, the saints, and angels. She is called the " Star of the sea, who supports the fallen state of mortals," " Mother of mercy, Our life and hope, Most gracious advocate. She graciously helps us to accomplish the work of our salvation, by her most powerful intercession." She is called, " Mirror of justice," " Seat of wisdom," " Cause of our joy," " Spiritual vessel," " Tower of David," " Ark of the covenant," " Gate of heaven," " Morning star," " Refuge of sinners," etc., etc.

If such expressions as these have any meaning at all, they ascribe to a human being attributes which belong to God alone.

VII.

WORSHIP OF THE VIRGIN

THE worship of Mary was originally only a reflection of the worship of Christ. As Mother of the Saviour of the world, the Virgin Mary unquestionably holds forever a peculiar position among all women. It is perfectly natural to associate with her the fairest traits of maidenly and maternal character, and to revere her as the highest model of womanly purity, love and piety.

The Roman Catholic Church, however, did not stop at this. After the middle of the fourth century, it overstepped the wholesome, Biblical limit, and transformed the "Mother of the Lord" into a "Mother of God." The veneration of Mary gradually degenerated into the worship of Mary. The origin of this worship may be traced to the apocryphal legends of her birth and death which were current during the second and third centuries. But the Christians of that day unanimously and firmly rejected them as fabulous and heretical. The deification of the Virgin Mary in the Roman Church was a slow process. First her perpetual virginity was asserted, then that her conception as well as her birth was supernatural. The third step was the decision of the Council of Ephesus, 481, that Mary was "the Mother of God." This decision, however, was rendered rather as a vindication of the divinity of Christ than as an exaltation of the glory of the Virgin. It had its origin in the Nestorian controversy, and was designed to combat an error touching the person of Christ, that Nestorius was accused of teaching. This decision was hailed as a triumph of

Orthodoxy, but it marks a distinct epoch in the progress of Mariolatry.

From this time the worship of Mary grew apace ; it agreed well with many natural aspirations of the heart. To paint the Mother of the Saviour an ideal woman, with all the grace and tenderness of womanhood, and yet with none of its weaknesses, and then to fall down and worship that which the imagination had set up, was what might easily happen. Evidence was not asked for. Perfection was becoming the Mother of the Lord, therefore she was perfect. She was adored and worshipped. She reigned as Queen in heaven, in earth, in purgatory, and over hell. Numerous churches and altars were dedicated to her worship. Even her images were divinely worshipped. and, in the prolific legends of the Middle Age, performed countless miracles, before some of which the miracles of the Gospel history grow dim. Prayers, hymns, and doxologies were allowed and prescribed to be addressed to her. The whole Psalter was transformed into a book of praise and confession to the Mother of Christ. This was done by Bonaventura, one of the great saints of the Church. I will give a specimen of his profane parody of these inspired Psalms—of the 51st : " Have pity upon me, O great Queen, who art called the Mother of Mercy, purify me from my iniquities." And so it runs throughout. The 149th Psalm is : " Sing a new song in honor of our Queen. Let the just publish her praises in their assemblies. Let the heavens rejoice in her glory ; let the isles of the sea and all the earth rejoice therein. Let water and fire, cold and heat, brightness and light, praise her ; let her praises resound in the triumphant company of the saints. City of God, place thy joy in blessing her, and let songs of praise continually be sung to her by thy illustrious and glorious inhabitants." The 19th Psalm—" The heavens declare thy glory O Virgin Mary, etc." And so on to the end of the book. In every instance the name of Mary is substituted for that of the Divine Being.

But of all the devotional writings on the worship of the Virgin, there are none that equal in bold blasphemy, " The Glories of Mary " by St. Liguori. I give only a few quotations, but they will show the character of the work, and give an idea of the religious reading the Church of Rome substitutes for the Word of God : " Mary is the Queen of the Universe, since Jesus is its King ; everything in heaven and on earth which is subject to God, is also under the empire of His most Holy Mother ! She is the Queen of Mercy alone ; she is a sovereign, not to punish sinners, but to pardon and forgive them. The kingdom of God consists in mercy and justice, the Lord has, as it were, divided it, reserving to himself the dominion of justice, and yielding to his Mother that of mercy." " God having created the heavens and the earth, made two great luminaries, the sun to rule the day, the moon to preside over the night. The former is a figure of Jesus Christ, whose splendid rays illumine the just who live in the day of grace ; the latter is typical of Mary, whose mild lustre illumines sinners amid the dreary night of sin. It is towards this propitious orb that he who is buried in the shades of iniquity should look. Having lost divine grace, the day disappears ; there is no more sun for him, but the moon is still in the horizon, let him address himself to Mary ;

under her influence thousands every day find their way to God." And so on throughout the entire book.

The necessary and inevitable tendency of Mary worship is to supersede the advocacy of our Divine Lord. She is exalted and kept in continual remembrance as the advocate of sinners. He is left in the background and practically ignored as the mediator between God and man. Protestants have but a faint idea of the character and extent of this worship among Roman Catholics. Ten prayers are offered to her where one is offered to our Lord. The Rosary and Litany of the Blessed Virgin are used more than any other prayers in the Prayer Book. The month of May is especially devoted to her worship, and as one has said, "*The controversy with Rome threatens more and more to resolve itself into the question, whether the creed of Christendom is to be based upon the life of Jesus or the life of Mary ; upon the canonical or the apocryphal gospels.*"

In the consideration of this subject, there are to every honest inquirer after the truth three questions that cannot be solved :

1. How can Mary and the departed saints hear at once the prayers of so many Christians on earth, unless they either partake of divine omnipresence or divine omniscience ? And is it not idolatrous to clothe creatures with attributes of the Godhead ? Augustine, the most philosophic thinker of his age, felt this difficulty and frankly conceded his inability to solve it.

This is one of the most difficult questions to answer in connection with the worship of the Virgin and the saints. Various theories have been devised and advanced, each one illogical, visionary, and diametrically

WORSHIP OF THE VIRGIN.

opposed to reason, and the entire tenor of Holy Scripture. The most rational theory of any is this, the mere statement of which is its own refutation : The Doctors of the Church admit that Mary is neither omniscient nor omnipresent, but they say that prayers offered to her, while she cannot hear them, are conveyed by God to her, and then she presents them to her Son, and He to the Father. Thus prayer to the Virgin Mary goes in a *circle* before it finally reaches the ear of the Infinite One. What a feeble, futile attempt to solve the incredible ! How can it be that men of thought are deluded by such thin vagaries. The truth is, however that after a dogma is adopted by the Church, that is by the Pope, their votaries are not allowed to *think*. As soon as a person begins to raise a question, or to entertain a doubt, he is assured that he is on dangerous ground. To doubt is a mortal sin.

2. As tradition is the principal factor in the Roman rule of faith, and as it is entirely silent in regard to the worship of the Virgin for the *first five centuries*, where is the authority for the innovation ?

And if this is a new doctrine, one that was not taught by Christ or his apostles, nor during the post-apostolic age, then the Roman claim that the Church is immutable, and that her teachings are the same in all ages, falls to the ground.

3. If the worship of Mary had the sanction of our Lord and His Apostles, how happens it that there is not a syllable in all the New Testament favoring such a practice ? Her name is not even once mentioned after the first chapter of the Acts. There are no allusions whatever either in the Gospels or the Epistles to the intercessions of the Virgin, saints, or angels.

VIII.

AT A PROTESTANT CHURCH

IN addition to the mental quickening, and the spiritual awakening that came to me from the daily searching of the Scriptures, and from intercourse with broad and pure-minded men, a strong desire sprang up in my heart to attend some non-Catholic service. I therefore inquired one day of Henry Henderson, with whom I was working, and a brother of James Henderson, my employer, if I might accompany him to church next Sunday. He was very glad to have me do so, and at the appointed time we met, and I went with him. It was in the afternoon. We went to the First Methodist Episcopal Church, the preacher being the pastor, Rev. John G. Gulick. As I had been taught from childhood to believe that Protestant worship was very bad—yea, *devilish*—and that it was a mortal sin to participate in such worship, my first impressions of such a service were very strange. The simplicity of the service, including the interior furnishing of the church, the dress of the officiating clergyman, and the language in which hymns were sung and prayers offered, was most striking. The minister wore plain, black clothes ; he helped himself, having no " altar boys " to wait on him ; and every word was in plain English, instead of Latin. The sermon from the text, " Redeeming the time, because the days are evil," was plain, practical, forceful, and timely. I remember it as though I had heard it but yesterday. He touched upon Spiritualism, as the Fox sisters were then living in Rochester, and the subject was at that time attracting much attention.

AT A PROTESTANT CHURCH.   45

That service was a revelation to me. It lifted the veil of prejudice that had been on my eyes concerning Protestant worship, and broadened my religious horizon. The Roman heirarchy are wise in prohibiting their people attending Protestant worship, for if that restriction were removed, there would be many more changes from one faith to the other.

In those days there were three public services in city churches on Sunday, and the service in the evening in the First Church was a prayer and conference meeting. I had a strong desire to attend one of these services, but as I spent Sunday at my father's, always remaining until Monday morning, I thus encountered a serious obstacle. The point was to find a reasonable excuse for returning to my boarding place on Sunday evening. Fortunately that winter there was a young man by the name of John B. Gough, a reformed drunkard, holding a series of temperance meetings in old Minerva Hall. His lectures attracted great attention, and I told my people I wanted to hear him. I went, and after hearing him awhile, I left, and went down to the Methodist meeting. After Mr Gough finished his course there was a young colored man who delivered a series of lectures on abolition in the same hall. He also was eloquent and popular, and drew large crowds on Sunday evenings, so I found no trouble in getting the consent of my parents to go to hear Frederick Douglass. I heard him, and also enjoyed the closing part of the prayer meeting.

It was in those meetings I received my first impressions touching the new life in Christ. The seed was there sown, or rather the incorruptible seed, the Word of God, which I had been hiding in my heart all these months, was there watered by the good Spirit, and the germ was kept alive, awaiting the coming fruitage. The spiritual singing, fervent prayers, and warm, heartfelt testimonies, concerning a present salvation were more persuasive and powerful than any argument that could be offered. I got an idea of what Paul meant when he told the young converts in Thessalonica that his gospel came to them not in word only, but also in power and in the Holy Ghost, and in much assurance.

My employer, Mr Henderson, evidently saw how the leaven of truth was working in my mind, for one day he asked me if I would like to go to a " class meeting." I told him I would. Now I did not know then what kind of a meeting that was. I had heard them talk about the " class meeting," but I thought it was a meeting of those in charge of classes in the Sunday School, or what we would call a " teachers' meeting." The meeting was held on Wednesday evening. On our way up to the class-room, Mr Henderson said to me, " Now, Sammie, they may ask you to speak to-night." " All right," I said, " I am ready to speak." We entered the well-lighted, plainly-furnished room, in which there were twenty or more persons seated. The meeting was in charge of George Evans, one of the most intelligent and best Bible scholars of that church. He opened the services with singing and prayer. He then spoke briefly of his experience in the divine life. I thought he spoke beautifully. Commencing at my right he next called upon each one to speak, and he replied, saying something that was helpful and comforting to each ; in the meanwhile someone would strike in and sing some of the most beautiful and touching things I had ever heard.

I was thoroughly delighted with the meeting. There was an influence or spirit that seized my heart and awakened, as it were, all the latent good desires and purposes, and I there resolved that I would lead a better life. But before the meeting was half over, I began to understand the force of Mr Henderson's remark as we entered the church, "They may want you to speak to-night." I began to realise that I was caught unawares. I thought, of course, that all the others came with their little speeches all ready, and there I was a stranger, with nothing to say, The exigency was serious. I saw no way out of the trap, for so I regarded it. The time was short in which to fix anything up. I had never had experience in that line before, and in my plight I hit upon this plan : as one and another spoke I selected an expression or sentence from different testimonies, exercising my judgment in taking the best offered. When my turn came, the leader said to me, "Now, my lad, and what have you to say ?" I did not think that I might decline, but I arose and spoke my little speech, which turned out to be the best of all, for it was made up of the choicest bits of all the testimonies I had heard.

I went once more after that, but never again until I had an experience of the life of God in my soul and could testify to the saving power of Jesus' blood applied through the operation of the Holy Spirit.

IX.

THE GIBRALTAR OF THE PAPACY

DURING the winter evenings of 1849 my mind and heart were all engrossed in the reading of the Word of God. I examined with care and prayer, to the limit of my ability, every Scripture passage pertaining to the distinctive doctrines of the Roman Church. My experience during those memorable months was a quest for the truth—it was a struggle for light and liberty—the light of revelation and the liberty of a son of God. I would read the old Book after work hours till midnight, and then as I wended my way to my home I would find myself instinctively crying out on the street, " O that I knew the right path ! O God, lead me to Thyself ! " The patriarch Job never voiced that prayer with deeper emphasis than did I during that anxious search : " O that I knew where I might find Him ! that I might come even to His seat ! "

Time and again my attention was directed to other books, but I always returned to the Bible as the true source of light and life. So that I can say, as did Paul, the Gospel I received was not after man, for I neither received it of man, neither was I taught it, but by the revelation of Jesus Christ, through his Word. A faithful report of the struggles of that winter would fill a volume. I can barely give an outline of them.

Having become thoroughly convinced that the Virgin Mary or the Saints had no power to hear or answer prayer, and that, therefore, all worship ascribed to them was vain and useless, unauthorised by the Word of God, unsanctioned by Jesus himself, and therefore meeting with his disapproval, I abandoned entirely all forms of worship pertaining to her or them. At this same time I was led to question the validity of auricular confession or confession to the ear of a priest. As I searched the Bible I found no warrant for it. James 5 : 16 proves too much : " Confess your faults one to another, and pray one for another, that ye may be healed." That enjoins a mutual confession. It has no reference whatever to confession to a priest. Matthew 18 : 18 is adduced : " Whatsoever ye shall bind on earth shall be bound in heaven, and whatsoever ye shall loose on earth shall be loosed in heaven." The words *bind* and *loose* are employed in the sense of obliging and dissolving, according to the customary phraseology of the Jews, when they would refer to anything that was *lawful* or *unlawful* to be done. The passage gave the Apostles authority to declare what was obligatory or dispensed with in the Jewish law ; and thus, by the authority of the Holy Spirit, of declaring what was to be retained or omitted in the Christian Church.

The text also in John 20 : 23 is brought forward for the purpose of establishing priestly absolution in the confessional : " Whosesoever sins ye remit, they are remitted unto them ; and whosoever sins ye retain, they are retained." The idea of auricular confession is not even hinted at in this passage. The thought is the Apostles received from the Lord the doctrine of reconciliation and condemnation. They who believed on the Son of God, according to their preaching, had their sins remitted, and they who would not believe were declared to be under condemnation. This is in accordance with Christ's commission, " He that believeth shall be saved, and he that believeth not shall be damned." And the ministers of Christ in every age have this power of remitting and retaining sins.

That no such power as the Roman priests claim was ever invested in the Apostles of Christ, or in the first ministers of Christianity, by the above cited commission, we have this indubitable proof : that they *never pretended to exercise such power*, but always ascribed the forgiveness of sins to God alone.

The primitive Church of Christ never believed that such power as is claimed by Roman Catholic priests was ever given by Christ to His ministers. They looked to God alone for this, as they thought Him alone qualified to bestow it.

As auricular confession is now the Gibraltar of the Papacy, and as there is a trend in certain Protestant high church circles to the practice of priestly confession, a glance at its rise and history may prove suggestive.

Auricular confession had its start under Pope Leo the Great in the 5th century. Previous to that time it had been the custom for notorious sinners to make a public confession before the congregation ; sometimes they would tell the ministers of their sins, and they would make the confession for them. But owing to the public scandal produced it was thought best to abandon the public confession, and a *silent*, prudent presbyter was appointed to receive the confessions. Pope Leo discouraged the ancient practice of public confession, and advocated with great zeal private confession to the priest alone.

Though the evil effects of the change were soon apparent in the general increase of crime, yet this was

THE GIBRALTAR OF THE PAPACY.

counterbalanced by the vast addition of influence which it gave the clergy. The conscience of the people was thus delivered over into the hands of the priests, the most secret acts and thoughts of individual imperfections were consigned to the torture of private inquisition and scrutiny ; and the first and corner-stone of the papal edifice was laid. However, there was no law requiring private confession until the 4th Council of Lateran, 1215. And until about this time the form of absolution was " *God absolves thee.*' **Afterward it was** changed to " *I absolve thee.*"

The more I read and thought and prayed on the subject, and especially reflected on my own experience in the confessional, the more clearly I became convinced that no priest on earth had power to forgive me my sins. I had been to confession time and again. I had gone through all the forms prescribed by the church and duly performed the penance enjoined, but never did I have any consciousness of sins forgiven ; nor did I receive through the sacrament (?) of penance any spiritual power wherewith I might resist the world, the flesh, and the devil.

I learned from the reading of the words of Jesus and his Apostles that if I confessed my sins to God, and exercised a sincere repentance, He would forgive me. I was encouraged by such promises as these : " If we confess our sins, He is faithful and just to forgive us our sins, and to cleanse us from all unrighteousness." " Let the wicked forsake his way, and the unrighteous man his thoughts, and let him return unto the Lord, and He will have mercy upon him ; and to our God, for He will abundantly pardon." " Come unto me all ye that labor and are heavy laden, and I will give you rest."

X.

TRANSUBSTANTIATION

DURING those months of Bible searching, and patient, prayerful thought, there was no doctrine of the Roman Church that so completely held my attention as that of Transubstantiation. As the word indicates, it is a change of one substance into another, a change of bread and wine into *the body and blood, the soul and divinity* of Jesus Christ. The doctrine of the Church of Rome is, that after the priest has pronounced the words of consecration, "*Hoc est corpus meum*," etc. (This is my body, etc.), what are seen to be bread and wine upon the altar are no longer bread and wine, but the real body and blood, soul and divinity of Jesus Christ. This wonderful change is produced by the use of these words, *Hoc est corpus meum*, and this, as Archbishop Tillotson says, led certain jugglers to call their sleight-of-hand tricks *hocus-pocus*, which is nothing but a corruption of the priest's *hoc est corpus*, by means of which he commands the whole substance of bread to be gone, and the real body of Christ to assume its place.

The bare statement of such a pretended miracle is enough to refute it, to the satisfaction of every person whose senses have any authority with his understanding.

In connection with my study of the simple narrative of the institution of the Lord's Supper, as found in the Gospels, I learned through Dr. Clark that our Lord conversed with his disciples, in all probability, in the Chaldaic, now the Syriac language, in which there is no term

TRANSUBSTANTIATION. 53

that expresses *to mean, signify, denote*—hence the Hebrews use a figure and say *it is*, for it *signifies*. There are numerous instances in the Bible illustrative of this. Thus the Apostle John, Rev. 1 : 20, uses the substantive verb as the Hebrews did—" The seven stars *are* the angels of the seven churches ; and the seven candlesticks *are* the seven churches." Who would imagine from this that the very substance of seven stars and seven candlesticks was converted into the very substance of the seven churches in Asia and of their seven ministers, as I suppose the word angel to mean.? Yet it must be so, upon the principle laid down by the Council of Trent, and maintained by all good Roman Catholics, upon the perversion of the words, " This *is* my body. ' The keystone of the Roman structure of transubstantiation rests upon the use of the substantive verb *is*, " This *is* my body,' which, according to the idiom of the language in which the words were spoken, could express no more than, this *signifies*, or *represents* my body.

In my reading I turned again to the words of Christ as they were spoken that night in the upper room, as he reclined at the table with the twelve. And I inquired, in what sense did the disciples understand these words : " And as they were eating, Jesus took bread, and blessed, and brake, and gave to the disciples, and said, ' Take, eat ; this is my body.' And He took the cup, and gave thanks, and gave to them, saying, ' Drink ye all of it ; for this is my blood of the New Testament, which is shed for many, for the remission of sins ? " Matt. 26 : 26-28. In the above passage the pronoun *it* is omitted. Why ? Because it is not found in the original but is supplied by the translators. They no doubt understood that the word *blessed* referred to the bread which our Lord took in His hand ; and if this were the meaning, their supplement would be correct ; but that, I apprehend. is a mistake. The word rendered " blessed " means. He gave thanks. " He took bread, and thanked God." So likewise in reference to the cup.

That Christ blessed God, and not the bread, is farther evident from the word which both Luke and Paul make use of to express what He did on that occasion. It is the very same word which Matthew uses in relation to the cup, and which signifies *gave thanks* ; and so our translators have rendered it, Luke 22 : 19, " And He took bread and *gave thanks* " ; and 1 Cor. 11 : 23-24, He " took bread, and when He had *given thanks*, He brake it, and said," etc. Here the pronoun *it* is properly supplied, because the action of breaking refers to the bread alone. Therefore the words *blessed* and *gave thanks* are expressions of precisely the same import, and God is the object of both.

Christ took bread into His hands, no doubt, and brake it, and said, " This is my body." The disciples were witnesses of His action and heard His words. Now I thought, how would we have understood Him had we been in the place of His disciples ? They were men like ourselves ; and as we would have felt and thought, they must have felt and thought. If we say they were men of other feelings and perceptions than we are, then we cannot judge of their testimony according to those rules of evidence which are applied to the " witness of *men*." They saw their Lord reclining at table, and taking bread in His hands ; they saw Him break the bread, they received the broken pieces into their own hands, and they ate them. They heard Him say, "This is my body"; but they expressed no surprise, which they would have done had they supposed that He was breaking His own body in pieces, with His own hands, and that they actually ate Him, as the Church of Rome teaches He is eaten every time the wafer is received. Such an unexpected operation would overwhelm any one of us with astonishment and dismay; and it would have done the same to the disciples had it actually taken place. They would have been, if possible, still more surprised if, after having eaten His body, they still saw Him reclining where He was, taking a cup into His hands, and telling them that this was His blood, which they were now to drink. Viewing the matter as it really was, that the bread and the wine *represented* His body and His blood, which were about to be broken and shed, everything is plain and intelligible, but viewing it in any other light, the thing is absurd and impossible. Had the disciples literally eaten the body of Christ, that which appeared and spoke to them afterwards must have been a mere phantom. Then there was no real sacrifice offered to God upon the cross; no real atonement for sin.

If, as the Roman Church claims, the eating of the bread and the drinking of the wine at the table in the upper chamber in Jerusalem by the eleven disciples was a real propitiatory or atoning sacrifice for the sins of the world, then was Christ offered up as a victim on Thursday night at the table before He was offered up the next day on the cross; and the disciples had eaten Him before He was crucified. That is the only logical construction of the Roman interpretation of the sacrament of the Lord s Supper. A plain, unvarnished statement of the case reveals the irrational absurdity of the dogma on which rests the entire fabric of the papacy.

Thus I saw that transubstantiation is not a mere harmless absurdity to be laughed at. It strikes at the root of the Christian religion. It subverts the doctrine of the cross of Christ ; and removes the only foundation on which a sinner can hope for the pardon of his sins, and the salvation of his soul.

In my Bible reading I found the Epistle to the Hebrews a rich storehouse of truth, touching this whole question. The writer of that inspired book insists that the death of Jesus Christ upon the cross was a perfect propitiatory sacrifice, offered up *once for all, for the sins of the world.* He stoutly maintains that the one offering is sufficient. If he were combating the pretentious claim of the Papacy, that in the mass the atoning work of Christ is repeated at the will of the priest, he could not be more explicit or clear in his declarations.

For example, in speaking of Christ, our great High Priest, he says : " For such a high priest became us, holy, guileless, undefiled, separated from sinners, and made higher than the heavens ; who needeth not daily, like those high priests (Jewish or Roman), to offer up sacrifices, first for his own sins, and then for the sins of the people : for this *he did once for all, when he offered up himself.* ' . . . " But Christ having come a high priest . . . through his own blood, entered in *once for all* into the holy place, *having obtained eternal redemption.*" " For Christ entered not into a holy place made with hands (like the little tabernacle on the altar in which the Roman priest puts the wafer) ; but into heaven itself, now to appear before the face of God for us; nor yet that he should *offer himself often* (as the priest in the mass); *but now once at the end of the ages* hath he been manifested to put away sin by *the sacrifice of himself.*" " And inasmuch as it is appointed unto men once to die . . . so Christ also, *having been once offered to bear the sins* of many."

In speaking of the coming Christ as the fulfiller of all the prophecies concerning sacrifices and offerings for sin he is represented as saying : " Lo, I am come to do tny will. By which will we have been sanctified through the offering of the body of Jesus Christ *once for all.* And every priest (Jewish or Roman) indeed standeth day by day ministering and offering oftentimes the same sacrifices, the which can never take away sins : but he, when he *had offered one sacrifice for sins* for ever, sat down on the right hand of God. . . . For by *one offering he hath perfected for ever* them that are sanctified." And finally under divine inspiration he declares : " *There is no more offering for sin* ! " Heb. chs. 9, 10.

But one more testimony is added, that of the Apostle John, in whose inspired writings such weighty emphasis is placed upon the sacrificial work of our great High Priest. John says : " He is the propitiation for our sins, and not for ours only but also for the sins of the whole world "; 1 Jo. 2 : 2, and for all time. Can anything be plainer than the above inspired declarations, that Christ was to be offered but *once*; and yet the Roman priests pretend to offer him on the altar in the mass, thousands of times every day !

The ninth and tenth chapters of the Hebrews furnish irrefragable proof-texts against the so-called miracle of transubstantiation and the pretended sacrifice of the mass.

As I read these inspired words : " BY ONE OFFERING HE HATH PERFECTED FOR EVER THEM THAT ARE SANCTIFIED," I felt the sandy foundation of the entire structure of transubstantiation and the mass give way, and my faith rested upon the sure Word of God : "*After He had offered one sacrifice for sins forever, sat down on the right hand of God.*"

XI.

THE SACRIFICE OF THE MASS

ACCORDING to Challoner's "Catholic Christian Instructed" the Mass is the liturgy of the Roman Catholic Church, and consists in the consecration of the bread and wine into the body and blood of Jesus Christ, and the offering up of the same body and blood to God, by the ministry of the priest, for a perpetual memorial of Christ's sacrifice upon the cross, and a continuation of the same to the end of the world.

In the service of the Mass is concentrated the whole mysterious fulness and glory of the Romish worship; and in it we find the center of the whole system. The term "Mass' came into use as early as the second century. Its origin would seem to be this : At the close of the service in the Latin or Western Church, when the holy communion was to be celebrated, and the ordinary ritual of the day was done, the priest addressing the people from the pulpit said, "Missa est," that is, "the congregation is dismissed"; and then followed the communion, immediately after the dismission of that part of the congregation who were not strictly communicants. From this expression "Missa est," being thus used previously to the sacrament of the Lord s Supper, this rite came to be called in very early times "Missa" and hence, in English, "The Mass." The word was retained in the liturgy of the English Church until 1552, when it was abandoned on account of the perverted sense attached to it by Roman Catholics.

To understand properly what is implied in the sacrifice of the Mass, we must bear in mind that the doctrine of the Church is that in the sacrament of the Eucharist are contained really and substantially, the body and blood, soul and divinity of our Lord Jesus Christ. "If anyone shall say that a true and proper sacrifice is not offered to God in the Mass ; or that what is to be offered is nothing else than giving Christ to us to eat, let him be accursed. If anyone shall say that the Mass is only a service of praise and thanksgiving, or a bare commemoration of the sacrifice made on the cross, and not a propitiatory offering, or that it only benefits him that receives it, and ought not to be offered for the living and the dead, for sins, punishments, satisfactions, and other necessities, let him be accursed." Dr. Challoner says that " there is a real change and *destruction* of the bread and wine, in their consecration, into the body and blood of Christ."

From these unequivocal statements it appears that nothing of the substance or essence of either the bread or wine remains. The sensible properties, or " accidents " as they term them, continue as they were. The form, color, taste, odor, the specific gravity, their chemical affinities, and their nutritive qualities remain the same. Our senses they claim are deceived.

Thus we see that transubstantiation is an essential element in the Mass, and is the very heart of Roman Catholic worship. Its importance cannot very well be overestimated. Moehler, the most philosophic and masterly writer on Romanism, represents it as the point in which all the differences between Romanists and Protestants converge.

THE SACRIFICE OF THE MASS.

No doctrine of the Church of Rome is more portentous or fruitful of evil consequences, and no doctrine of that Church is more entirely destitute of even a semblance of Scriptural support. The words of Christ, "This do in remembrance of me," are made to mean, "Offer the sacrifice which I myself have just offered." These words constituted the twelve apostles and their successors, priests. The Council of Trent even anathematized all who do not put that preposterous interpretation upon it. Thus the Roman Catholic Church has changed the Eucharist, which was a *thank-offering*, into the Mass, which is a *sin-offering*.

In the writings of Justin Martyr we have a minute description of a sacramental service celebrated in the second century. It bespeaks the primitive simplicity of Christian worship, and presents a most striking contrast to the Romish Mass.

The question concerning the "*real presence*" was not agitated in the Eastern Church until the second Council of Nice in A.D. 787. About the year 820, Rathbert, abbot of Corbie, wrote a book to show that Christ changed the bread and wine into the real body and blood, as born of the Virgin Mary. But this view was regarded as strange and heretical, and a fierce controversy ensued. The most noted divines of the Church were arrayed on both sides, showing that it was simply an *opinion* not an *article of faith*. Finally, at a private Council held at Rome, A.D. 1050, under Nicolas II., it received a vote of endorsement. Afterward in 1215, at the Council of Lateran, it was formally accepted as a doctrine of the Church. Now for the first time the word " transubstantiation " finds a place in the Roman creed ;

and after a lapse of nearly twelve centuries, the Church is authoritatively informed that every time the elements are consecrated, the Son of God in his humanity and divinity appears in the fingers of the priest.

Let it be borne in mind also that this power, if it exists at all, is necessarily unlimited. All the wine that may be contained in a cellar, all the bread that may be found in a baker's shop, the priest may, by a few words, convert into the body and blood of Christ. Yea, by one act, he may create a million Christs, for every particle of the bread broken off contains a whole Christ.

But even the decision of the Council of Lateran did not settle the matter, for from that time until the Council of Trent in the sixteenth century, it was a debated question among the great doctors of the Church whether the doctrine was taught in Holy Scripture, and some of the ablest theologians of the Church, including even distinguished Cardinals, conceded that the proof for the dogma must be found outside the Word of God.

The worship of the wafer was not known until 1216, and it was not until the following year that Pope Honorius III. ordered the elevation of the Host at a certain part of the service of the Mass. The genesis and growth of this monstrous absurdity forms a most interesting historic study. Fortunately for the cause of truth, its rise and development can be easily traced; and its history is its strongest refutation. We can readily see where the seed of the dogma was sown in the mystical, hyperbolic, figurative language and interpretation indulged in by the Ante-Nicene fathers. The germs of the doctrine appear in Cyprian about the middle of the third century in connection with his high-churchly doctrine of the clerical priesthood. Even in Justin Martyr and Irenaeus we meet with the unscriptural conception of the Lord's Supper as a sacrifice ; at first as a sacrifice of thanksgiving, but soon as a sacrifice of expiation.

Intimately connected with the history of the Mass, is that of the liturgies. Though Romanists ascribe some of their oldest liturgies to St. James, St. Mark, and some of the post-apostolic fathers, yet it is an unquestioned fact, that there are no traces of liturgical writings previous to the fourth century. The Roman liturgy now in use is ascribed by tradition, in its main features, to the apostle Peter ; but it cannot be historically traced beyond the middle of the fifth century. It has without doubt grown slowly to its present form. It is an imposing ceremony, being arranged for dramatic effect, and is well designed to impress the ignorant, and hold the attention of the learned. Everything connected with it, from the vestments worn by the priest to the culminating act, the elevation of the Host, has a symbolic meaning. The first article that the priest puts on is a small white linen cloth, placed on the shoulders, close to the neck. This is the *amyct*, and represents the muffling of our Saviour's face by the Jews. The girdle signifies the cords by which he was bound. The full outer vestment, the purple garment with which he was clothed in mockery in the court of Pontius Pilate—and so with every article worn in the performance of the ceremony. The altar represents Calvary ; the linen clothes, the winding sheets ; the silver plate, the stone rolled against the door of the sepulchre ; and the candles the light of the Spirit or of faith. The colors employed also have symbolic meanings, likewise every movement and gesture of the officiating priest from the time he takes his position at the foot of the altar to the close of the ceremony. The service being performed in Latin also imparts to it an air of mystery. It is addressed to the senses, through the display of lights, the beauty of the vestments, the profusion of flowers, the incense and the music. The importance which the Church attaches to this service is illustrated by the fact that attendance at Mass once on Sunday, if in health, is obligatory upon all Catholics. This accounts for the large attendance at public worship in Catholic churches. Non-attendance at Mass, if able to go, is classed with mortal sins endangering the soul with eternal punishment. The Mass is also very intimately connected with the Treasury of the Church. Masses, for the dead, are offered up daily in every church in Christendom ; and for every such service a handsome sum is required.

XII.

REACHING A CRISIS

AS the result of my earnest and sincere searching of the Word of God for the months that were past, I became thoroughly satisfied that I could no longer hold to the distinctive teachings of the Roman Catholic Church. I had given up the worship of Mary, and the saints and angels. I could no longer believe that the priest had power to forgive me my sins. As to Transubstantiation and the sacrifice of the Mass, I could find no support for them in Scripture. So, likewise, with the other specific tenets of the Church ; but I mention these especially because they are the pivotal doctrines of the Church of Rome. If either one is void of a solid Scriptural foundation, then the entire fabric collapses and falls to the ground.

Owing to my change of views and unsettled state of mind, I could no longer go to confession. It was now Lent. According to the custom and teaching of the Church, every good Catholic goes to confession and communion during this holy season. If he allows Easter to pass without attending to such duties, he should regard himself as self-excommunicated. Heretofore, I had been so devoted in such observances, prompting other members of the family to their church duties, that my neglect or delay in going to confession occasioned remark, and led my father to remind me of my duty. In reply I always made some excuse, until at last father evidently became alarmed and pressed the matter so closely that I had either to declare to him my change of views or promise to go to confession. I did not have courage to do the former, so I promised him I would do the latter. He asked me, " When ? " I said, a week from the next Saturday. The die was cast. Go I must. What should I do ? As I thought the matter over, I made up my mind I would go and make a clean breast of it and tell the priest frankly my state of mind. The intervening days were a time of earnest, honest thought, sincere heart-searching and prayer, and the most thorough reading of the Word of God. I had no one to consult. I did not venture to open my mind to my employer. I had no comrades or associates among Protestants. It was a solitary struggle of a sincere soul after the truth. As I thought the matter over, I decided upon this method of procedure : I would go to the priest and unburden my heart in regard to the worship of the Virgin Mary. I therefore thoroughly memorised those passages concerning the fact that Jesus Christ is our only advocate or intercessor, so that I could use them to good effect.

At length the Saturday afternoon came on which I was to fulfil my promise. I went to St. Mary s Church on St. Paul Street. I entered the confessional, a little room that once had been a Methodist class room ; for the building had formerly been owned by the Methodists, and some of the most distinguished men in Methodism had preached in it—Drs. John Dempster, Glezen Filmore, and others. Father Carroll was the priest. I knelt at his feet. I had to go through the preliminary forms before I came to the act of confession. I made the sign of the cross. I repeated the *confiteor* or form of confession, which is as follows : " I confess to Al

REACHING A CRISIS.

mighty God, to blessed Mary, ever a Virgin, to blessed Michael the Archangel, to blessed John the Baptist, to the holy apostles, Peter and Paul, to all the saints and to thee, Father (the priest) that I have sinned exceedingly, in thought, word and deed, through my fault, through my most grievous fault : therefore I beseech the blessed Mary, ever a Virgin, the blessed Michael, the Archangel, the blessed John the Baptist, the holy apostles, Peter and Paul, all the saints and thee, Father, to pray to the Lord our God for me."

Having gone through this form, I then entered upon the task of the hour. I said to him : " Father, I can no longer pray to the Virgin Mary." His first word in reply was, " Ah, you have been reading the Protestant Bible." I told him I had been reading the Bible, but I did not know whether it was Catholic or Protestant, and I could find no authority in it for worshipping her. Then followed such a scene as I have not language to describe. When I first knelt at his feet I trembled for fear, but I had not been there long when all fear was gone, and I was full of courage, and had great liberty in upholding the position I had taken. I was a long time on my knees before him. As nearly as I can recall it was about two hours. The position that I took was that Jesus was our only advocate, and that through him we might approach the Father. And since he had said so plainly, " Come unto Me," to allow anyone, his mother, or saint, or angel to come between him and us would be to dishonour him and detract from his glory. In proof of all this I brought forward three witnesses. I reserved their testimonies to the last. First the apostle John : " If any man sin, we have an advocate with the Father,

Jesus Christ the righteous," no mention there of Mary, though she had spent her last days with the beloved disciple. I next produced Paul: "There is one God and one mediator between God and man, the man Christ Jesus." The priest's reply to that was so silly that a child could detect its weakness, "Yes," said he, "Paul says there is one mediator, but he does not say there is no more than one." I reserved what I deemed my strongest proof-text to the last. Peter, I had been taught to believe, was the first pope. Surely Father Carroll will accept his testimony. In speaking of Jesus, Peter says, "Neither is there salvation in any other: for there is none other name under heaven given among men, whereby we must be saved!"

As the interview closed I felt that I had gained a great victory, and I arose from my knees strengthened rather than shaken in my faith. And yet, Father Carroll and I agreed perfectly on one point—"Well, my lad," said he, "I am sorry for you, but in your present state of mind I cannot absolve you from your sins." In that we thought alike, for I had no idea he could forgive me in my present state of mind or any other!

The next morning, which was Sunday, I went for the first time, in daylight, except that first afternoon, to a Protestant Church.

In the afternoon, when at my father's, the question was asked where I had been to church, as we did not always attend the same Catholic Church. Now the crisis was reached. I said, "I have been to the Methodist Church." "What!" said father. "Yes," said I, "and if you would read the Bible, you would be a Methodist, too, father." That was an impulsive and unwise remark. There were present in the room my father, mother, and my sister Eliza. The scene that followed is indescribable ; the tears and pleadings and prayers were pathetic in the extreme. In due time my father got my cap, placed it on my head, took me firmly by the arm and marched me off to the priest. When we reached a certain corner we came to a halt. He was for taking me over to St. Mary's. Having had an interview with Father Carroll the day before, I did not wish to see him so soon again. So as I was stubborn and would not yield, he took me to St. Patrick's Church, and for an hour Father O'Reilly talked to me. But to tell the truth his words did not fall with much weight upon my mind, especially when I recalled his intemperate habits, and how offensive his breath had been to me while in the confessional.

* * * * * * *

Now follows a passage in my experience that I would fain omit. For twenty years I never told it when relating the story of my conversion. I was ashamed to. For, I thought, since no one would appreciate the situation, it would reveal a great weakness in me.

The bald facts are these : Every influence or means that love or zeal or paternal devotion could devise to force or draw me back was used. Day and night I was followed up, at the shop, at my lodgings, at my father's home. There was no respite from the ceaseless, importunate entreaties, the fearful threats, and weightier than all the tears and breaking heart of my mother. Although convinced of the errors of Roman Catholicism, I had not met with a change of heart. I had no just comprehension of the nature and necessity of the new birth as taught by Jesus to Nicodemus. I had, therefore, no divine strength or inner spiritual power to uphold and enable me to meet this incoming tide of opposition. There was nothing to bind me to Protestants. I had no friends among them. All I cared for was to save my soul. Could I not do it in the old Church ? The struggle continued day after day. I didn't mind my dear father's violent threats. He might have disowned me, and turned me out of house and home ; I could have stood that. But when mother, with pale cheeks and breaking heart, would clasp me to her bosom and exclaim, " O Samuel, Samuel, don't you know you are breaking my heart ? " I did not have the strength to resist, and so without re-examining the subject, but just smothering my honest convictions, I went right back and that summer became a more zealous Catholic than ever. I became a teacher in the Sunday School. I read all the devotional books I could get hold of. I made all the necessary preparations to return to Ireland and place myself under the care of my uncle, to be educated for the priesthood. I attended the Church of the Immaculate Conception of the Blessed Virgin Mary on Cornhill. I was one of its first members

On the same street, immediately opposite, is the Cornhill Methodist Episcopal Church that was organised some years after this. I was one of the charter members of that church also !

XIII.

THE DARKNESS BEFORE DAWN

THE summer months had passed. It had been an eventful season. My mental and spiritual conditions were exceptional. I intended to be honest. The change in my religious views and attitude had been forced upon me by circumstances. My controlling thought and the overmastering desire of my heart was to save my soul. I was intensely in earnest. I endeavoured to lead a good life. My love for the Word of God had not waned. I carried with me constantly my small copy of the New Testament, and even in church, as I knelt beside my father, and as he read his prayer book, I read the words of Jesus in the Gospels.

I entertain a vivid recollection of a remarkable experience I had one Sunday afternoon while reading the New Testament. It was a summer day. I sat on the doorstep of my boarding-house, reading the First Epistle of Peter. I had begun at the first and had gotten to the fourth chapter, when my attention was rivetted, my conscience aroused, and my heart stirred as never before as I read these words : " For the time is come that judgment must begin at the house of God : and if it first begin at us, what shall the end be of them that obey not the Gospel of God ? And if the righteous scarcely be saved, where shall the ungodly and the sinner appear ? "

That last question went like an arrow from God's quiver to my heart. I closed the book. I could read no further. And for days those words kept ringing in my heart ; they were quick and powerful.

My dear father, I think, rejoiced with trembling. He must have indulged in some slight suspicions of my steadfastness, for he always accompanied me to church, never suffering me to go alone.

The winter before this there used to come into the shop where I worked a young Irishman by the name of William McDermott. He was then about 28 years of age. He had been brought up a Roman Catholic, but in early life was converted to Bible Christianity. He was a remarkable character and was chosen of God, I believe, to deliver me from the thraldom of error. McDermott was bright and brainy. He had made a thorough study of the Bible and of church history. He had a wonderful memory, a clear head, and an exceptional command of language. He never entered the shop without taking up the Bible and reading and expounding some portion of it. Like Apollos, he was eloquent and mighty in the Scriptures. He had moved out of the city for the summer, and when he returned in the fall Mr. Henderson told him about me and how I had gone back to the old church. He came to the shop one morning and opened a conversation on the subject of religion. We became so deeply interested that we did not go to dinner. I held my own the best I could, though not with great success, for he possessed such a masterful knowledge of the whole subject. After supper he returned, and we talked until nine o'clock. He came the next day, when he did most of the talking. The third day he was again on hand, and he now had the field to himself. The result of that three days' conference was the complete removal of the film that had covered my mental vision for the past few months and such a thorough indoctrination in the fundamental truths of Christianity as I had never had before. In addition to a review and expose of the errors of Rome, he dwelt especially upon the necessity of the new birth. He expounded and unfolded so clearly the third chapter of John's Gospel that a profound impression was made upon my mind. He told me plainly and frankly that I might as well stay where I was as to join any of the Protestant churches unless I experienced the new birth. As he talked, especially on the third day, the Spirit of God wrought with power upon my heart, and I purposed to open the subject again for examination. In addition to the revival of the old convictions touching the errors of Rome, I was led to realize that I was a sinner and must needs experience the washing of regeneration and the renewing of the Holy Ghost.

But O the days and weeks of mental anguish and soul travail that followed ! I was driven to and fro by conflicting currents of thought. What was I to do ? What about this new birth ? What of this experimental religion ? I knew what I should have to encounter if I made another move outward from the old church. I must count the cost. I must know the ground whereon I stood. I was at a crisis. I said to myself, I wish I knew of someone I could trust who has had an experience in this spiritual life, someone who could give an impartial testimony on the whole subject. All at once it flashed upon my mind, Why here he is by your side, Henry Henderson, the man with whom you are working. Sure enough. Now I knew enough about Methodists to know that they backslide; and I knew that this man had been a Christian before coming to the city, but he had backslidden and no longer made a profession of religion. I had, however, great confidence in him. I knew he would tell me the truth about the matter; so one day I broke the silence by asking him if this religion they talked about down at the Methohist church was genuine. The question touched a tender spot. It went like an arrow to his heart. It took him about fifteen minutes to make answer to my query. He told of his conversion in Bucks County, Pa., how happy he was in his first love, and then how he came to Rochester and fell away from the faith. As he talked the tears coursed down his cheeks, and he gave a testimony that might have graced a revival meeting. We were all alone. While he testified and wept, my heart was moved, and I resolved then, God helping me, I would seek the Lord until I found Him.

Mr. Henderson went home that night and told his wife, who was also a backslider, that when sinners were coming to them to inquire the way of life it was time they changed their course and came back to God.

The testimony of this man produced a wonderful impression upon my mind. It called to remembrance those testimonies touching Christian experience that I had heard the previous winter in the class and prayer meeting. I had been taught to believe in the Roman Church that one could not know that his sins were forgiven and that the love of God was shed abroad in the heart. But here were men and women whose testimony would be received in any court of justice who bore witness to the fact of experimental religion, and I had also learned from the reading of the Bible that such experience was in accordance with its teachings. I had become quite familiar with the writings of the Apostle John, and I learned from him that there is no doubt that we may know that we have passed from death unto life. And as I read Paul's writings and the Psalms I saw that the personal experimental element is a distinctive feature of all those portions of Holy Scripture.

Bearing in mind those facts concerning my early experience, I have always been impressed with the importance of Christian testimony to the verities of the life of God in the soul. The Holy Spirit evidently uses such means for the purpose of glorifying Christ and winning men to the truth. Ye are my witnesses, saith the Lord.

XIV.

THE MORNING BREAKS

IT was the 28th day of November, 1849, Thanksgiving Day. There were but two Methodist Churches then in Rochester, the First, and St. John's, now Asbury. The Thanksgiving service in which both churches united was at St. John's, Rev. D. D. Buck, pastor. I went to church that morning with the great thought of God filling mind and heart. Before the sermon, as the pastor announced that, that night at the First Church, a series of revival meetings would commence, and that a young man, fresh from college, Rev Martin C. Briggs, would preach, I said in my heart "God helping me, I will begin to seek the Lord to night."

When evening came I went to church. The house was filled. I sat on the back seat. Although the preacher was eloquent I have no recollection of a word he said, of text or sermon. I was thinking only of myself and of my sins, the important step I was about to take, and the inevitable results that would follow. The sermon over, and the invitation given to penitents to go forward to the mourner's bench, I did not wait for anyone to invite me, personally. I started at once and hastened to the front. I made fast time in the way of the Lord ! The work of my awakening, conviction, and conversion, from first to last, was the effect of the Word and the Spirit of God. In humility and self-abasement I could say in the language of Paul that the gospel which I received was not after man, " for I neither received it

THE MORNING BREAKS. 77

of man, neither was I taught it, but by the revelation of Jesus Christ," through His Word.

In this brief narrative of my conversion from a religion of form to one of power, I wish to magnify the Word of God, honor the Spirit of God, and glorify the Christ of God. Of course I recognise, with gratitude to God, the human means that were employed in my case. As the dying testimony of Stephen and the prayer of Ananias were instrumental in ushering Saul of Tarsus into the light of the new life, so, likewise, did the Lord own the tireless efforts of Henderson in enlisting my interest in the Holy Scriptures, and the timely interposition of McDermott in removing the bandages of unbelief that for a while had bound my eyes. Nevertheless, I could say, " It is the Lord's doings, and it is marvelous in our eyes," and " Not unto us, not unto us, but unto Thy name give glory."

Having gone forward for the prayers of the Church, I knelt down, and fervent and importunate prayer was offered in my behalf. I felt that I had entered a warm heavenly atmosphere. I love to think of those godly men and women who gathered around me that first night, and following nights, and prayed for the " little Catholic boy." The experience of the following five days, while seeking the Lord, stands out in memory as distinct and fresh as the occurrence of yesterday. While a " seeker " my experience was peculiar, if not exceptional. Though burdened with a deep sense of sin, for I knew what it was to be convicted of sin by the Holy Spirit, yet I was happy in the thought of what I expected to receive. For I was not making an experiment. I knew whom I was seeking, and I was sure I would find Him. I therefore rejoiced in hope. I did not seek "religion." I was not trying to be a Protestant. I was seeking "the Kingdom of God and His righteousness." Yea, I was in search of the King, Himself. I went home that night with a light though burdened heart. I was full of prayer. I sought Him even in the night. I awoke in the morning and my waking thoughts were of Him. And so it was day after day and night after night, from Thursday until the following Tuesday. I was an obedient son in the gospel. I did whatever I was told to do I spoke in the meeting, telling of my desires and purposes and confessing my sins. I prayed for myself and humbled myself before the Lord. And yet I did not experience that change of heart of which I had heard Christians speak. Tuesday night came. The interest in the meetings by this time had become deep and general. There were many others beside myself who were inquiring the way of life. After a season of prayer, the "seekers" were asked to speak. I quickly arose and told how I felt. My remarks evidently made a deep impression, for one of the ministers present, Rev. Mr. Buck, arose and said, "That little lad is within a step of the Kingdom." At once, hope sprang up in my heart, for I had no idea that I was so near. I had been accustomed to do penance after confession to the priest for thirty days at a time, and then not get relief, and to think I was just on the threshold of the Kingdom gave me new courage. Mr. Buck then went on to explain the way of faith, telling me how I might take this last step. He made it very clear. As there are but two steps from self and sin to Christ and salvation : repentance toward God, and faith in our

Lord Jesus Christ, he was satisfied that I had taken the
first step; that I had broken with the world and my
old sinful life, and that all required now was an act of
saving faith in my living Redeemer. I would most
gladly then, ere I entered the light, have gone to the
stake rather than abandon the search. I think he must
have unfolded the 10th Chapter of that letter that Paul
once wrote to the Church of Rome. I am quite sure he
did. There is nothing more apt or appropriate in the
entire Word of God. " The Word is nigh thee, even in
thy mouth, and in thy heart : that is the word of faith ;
that if thou shalt confess with thy mouth the Lord
Jesus, and shalt believe in thine heart, thou shalt be
saved. For with the heart man believeth unto righteousness ; and with the mouth confession is made unto
salvation." While he spake the word, the Spirit gently
opened the door of my heart. We at once bowed in
prayer again, and my knees hadn't touched the floor
before the light dawned, the day star arose in my heart.
The burden was lifted, and I was at rest in the Lord.
I heard no voice of man saying, " I absolve thee from
thy sins," but I felt the touch of the Divine hand of
my great High Priest, the Bishop and Shepherd of my
soul that gave me full and free remission of all the past.
It was an unconditional surrender on my part ; it was
an abundant pardon on His. " With Thee there is
forgiveness, that Thou mayest be feared." " Though
your sins be as scarlet, they shall be as white as snow ;
though they be red like crimson, they shall be as wool.''

Immediately on rising from our knees, I testified to
what God had done for me. There was great rejoicing
among the saints. The evidence of the great change

wrought was clear and satisfactory. I could say in the language of the Apostle John, "The darkness is past, and the true light now shineth;" and with the blind man whom Jesus healed, "One thing I know, that, whereas I was blind, now I see!" I understood then what Paul meant when he said, "The Spirit Himself beareth witness with our spirit, that we are the children of God." I was so happy in this new relation I felt I was "no more a stranger and foreigner, but a fellow-citizen with the saints, and of the household of God;" and that my faith rested upon the foundation of the apostles and prophets, Jesus Christ himself being the chief corner stone. I therefore went home, singing in my heart :

> "Oh, happy day, that fixed my choice
> On Thee, my Saviour and my God!
> Well may this glowing heart rejoice,
> And tell its raptures all abroad."

XV.

TRIED AS BY FIRE

I WAS boarding at this time with Henry Henderson, whose testimony while in a backslidden state was one of the means that Infinite Wisdom used for my enlightenment. Both he and his wife were reclaimed about the time of my conversion, and a happy family we were. The family altar was at once established, and walking in the fear of the Lord and in the comfort of the Holy Ghost we were edified.

But though I was very happy in my new experience, I had counted the cost and I knew what would be the outcome when my parents and friends learned of the change. a great burden, therefore, rested daily upon me. Night after night I went to my father's, intending to tell them, but my heart failed me. If the question had been put to me, I would have confessed my faith though it might have cost me my life, for I was strong in the Lord and in the power of His might. It was two weeks, however, after my conversion before I could muster courage to tell them what I feared would break their hearts.

As I left my boarding place one night Mr. Henderson and his wife both said to me : "God bless you, and give you courage to-night." I made my visit at home, and as was her custom, my mother accompanied me to the corner of the next street. As we walked along I broke the news to her. We stood still on the walk. She embraced me and exclaimed, "O Samuel, I feared this!" The experience of that evening hour is too sacred to be put on record. Indeed, language would fail me in the attempt. We parted in sadness, and the next day I was summoned home. My father felt very bitter towards Mr. Henderson, as he thought he had been the means of my conversion, and he would, therefore, no longer permit me to remain with him. For four weeks I was kept in the house, my father forbidding me to go anywhere. He thought that by keeping me away from the Methodists and their meetings there would be more hope of my return to the old faith. It was a great mistake on his part, but it was a special advantage to me, for I had nothing to do during the day but read my Bible and hymn book, which I carried with me constantly so that I grew daily in the knowledge of our Lord and Saviour Jesus Christ. However, while I obeyed him to the letter during the day, I felt that I ought to make an exception at night. So before he returned from his work I would have an early supper, slip out the back door, and make my way to the evening service. The revival meeting was progressing with power, and every service I attended was to me a special means of grace. I made the most of every opportunity. I needed no urging to take part in the "after meeting," or social part of the service. I was so eager to tell what wonderful things the Lord had done for me, and I was so happy in my new experience I was usually the first to testify to the grace of God. The daily trials I encountered at home through the incessant efforts put forth by my family and friends intensified my zeal and led me to lean harder on the everlasting arms of my Divine Redeemer. I was, therefore, joyful in hope, patient in tribulation, and instant in prayer. I knew something of the experience that Paul said the young converts of Thessalonica had who " received the Word in much affliction, with joy of the Holy Ghost."

It would be impossible to recall, at this date, the trying experiences of those weeks. Some of them were of an exceptional character. I always dreaded meeting my father upon my return from the evening service. He was very affectionate toward his children, but his wrath waxed hot against the Methodists, and he made many threats respecting myself which were never put into execution, but which gave me the keenest anguish of heart. During those days I found much in the Epistles of Peter to comfort and inspire with hope. Especially adapted to my case were such words as the following : " Beloved, think it not strange concerning the fiery trial which is to try you, as though some strange thing happened unto you ; but rejoice, inasmuch as ye are partakers of Christ's sufferings ; that, when His glory shall be revealed, ye may be glad also with exceeding joy."

The trying experiences of those four weeks reached a climax one night upon my return from meeting. It was the severest test of my faith in those early days, as it proved to be the heaviest strain upon my feelings and my natural affections. As I have thought of it since I have always entertained the belief that father and mother planned the onset as a final effort to win or coerce me back to my former faith. At all events, nothing was left undone, that night, to accomplish this end. Not one of the family retired. It was an all-night scene. Entreaties, expostulations, pleadings, alternating with threatenings and warnings, mingled with tears and prayers, first in one room and then in another, up-stairs and down-stairs,—thus passed the live-long night. That was a crucial time. There was one hour during that dreadful night that was decisive. My mother and I were up-stairs. She held my head in her arms as the hot tears fell upon me, and with all the tenderness of her great loving heart she begged me to return. As we stood there I thought and prayed. I said to myself, Can I not go back and save my soul? That was all I cared for. I thought, however, of the wonderful blessing I had received during the past few weeks, of the peace and joy in believing, such as I had never had through the absolution of the priest or the reception on my tongue of the wafer in the sacrament; and there and then I said God helping me I will "stand fast in the liberty wherewith Christ hath made me free." The victory was gained, and I could say with Paul, "In all these things we are more than conquerors through Him that loved us."

After the experiences of this night my father evidently became satisfied that there was no use in exercising any further restraint upon me, so he allowed me to go to work for a very excellent man, Mr. Armitage, a member of the Presbyterian Church. While with him I had the great pleasure of hearing the Rev. Dr. Nicholas Murray, the author of "Kirwan's Letters to Bishop Hughes," preach. Dr. Murray had been converted from Roman Catholicism at about the same age as myself, and hearing him preach was a great privilege and means of grace.

The aim and scope of this brief narrative forbids my entering into further details of my experience after this. I could easily fill a volume. While writing I have kept

TRIED AS BY FIRE.

my pen constantly under restraint. I desire this brochure to reach at least a million readers. Therefore its brevity and compactness. I have made no attempt to cover the whole ground or to give all my reasons for leaving Rome and embracing Bible Christianity. If I have given one solid reason, it suffices. For Rome claims infallibility, and a weak link in the chain is, therefore, fatal.

As soon as I was converted I had a strong desire for an education. I had not been at school from the time I was ten years of age, having earned wages from that early period in my life. At the time of my conversion I was earning good wages for a boy, all of which I gave to my father, with the exception of a small sum, which he allowed me to retain every week. That I put in the bank against going to school. During the summer I talked with my parents about the Seminary at Lima, N. Y., and got their consent to my going there the fall following my conversion. They did not know, however, that it was a Methodist school. When I got ready to go I had $35.00 in the bank. Thirty of that I gave my father for the family and went to Lima with $5.00 in my pocket. I took care of the halls and recitation rooms for my tuition and worked Saturdays for my board. Miss Ellen Green, afterward the wife of the Rev. Dr. Martin C. Briggs of California, was the preceptress. When my father learned that the Seminary was under Methodist patronage he sent for me to come home. I obeyed him, and went to work again for the family, giving my father all my earnings until I was twenty years of age, at which time he released me, and I then went to the Collegiate Institute in Rochester. I paid my tuition, which was $40.00 a year, by taking care of the schoolroom, and paid for my board by doing chores morning and night about three miles from school.

Of nine children I am the only one who ever left the old Church. Two of my sisters became Sisters of Charity; one of them is now living and is connected with St. Vincent's Asylum, Albany, N. Y.

My mother died in Rochester, at the age of 45 years. She was a lovely character, being regarded as a very saintly woman by those who knew her. We had a great many talks together on the subject of religion. Her last illness continued six months. During that time the Sisters of Charity came often to see her for their own spiritual benefit, so highly did they esteem her Christian life. She belonged to one of their societies, something pertaining to the Virgin Mary. Before death she was clad in a special garb. But, strange to say, I never heard her during her last illness mention the Virgin Mary. All her talk was about the Saviour, and her last words were, " Jesus will soon come and take me away." I have no doubt that she died trusting in Him who is our only Advocate with the Father.

She died on Friday night, and was buried on Sunday. My eldest sister, who lived in Canada, had come to her burial. This was the first time she had seen me since my conversion. She was a woman of strong prejudices, and could not endure the thought of my having changed my faith. The funeral was in the afternoon. In the morning the entire family went to mass. A special effort was put forth to induce or compel me to go also. I felt, however, that I could not conscientiously do so, and I therefore stoutly resisted their importunities.

TRIED AS BY FIRE.

My sister's last plea for my going was this: "I should think you would pay enough respect to your dead mother to go to church and offer up a prayer for the relief and rest of her poor soul." I replied by saying, " I have more confidence than you in my mother's piety. I believe she is at rest in heaven, and, therefore, does not need our prayers; while you think she is suffering in purgatory."

XVI

MOTHER HULL IN EVIDENCE

NEXT door to us in Ireland lived a godly Methodist family by the name of Hull. Their house was the home and preaching place of the itinerant minister, whenever he came round on his circuit, and I well remember that on every other Tuesday evening, in winter and in summer, the preacher could be seen passing our door on his way to his appointment at our neighbors' house. They had a large family of children, eleven in all, and they were all professing Christians except the oldest son. I knew he was not one, because when the meetings were in progress, he would be outdoors with the Catholic boys and others, making sport of the loud praying and singing within. This I could not then understand, and it made a deep impression upon my young mind.

Notwithstanding the fun the neighboring children used to make of the Methodist meetings, my parents had a profound respect for the family. They were not only excellent neighbors, but they proved to be true and lasting friends. When we emigrated to America there were none who showed a deeper or more sincere grief at our departure than these zealous Methodists. The friendship which existed between the two families was not formed or sustained through any compromise of principles on the part of either. Each was equally strong in its own faith. And yet so strong were the

MOTHER HULL IN EVIDENCE.

ties of real friendship that for some time after we came to America, correspondence was kept up between my mother and Mrs Hull, which, all things considered, was quite remarkable.

Shortly after my conversion, my mother and I were having an earnest conversation upon the subject of religion. I told her my experience and enlarged upon the joy and blessedness of the new life in Christ which I had found. I urged upon her the necessity of the new birth. I rehearsed to her the interview between Jesus and Nicodemus, and quoted the words of Jesus, "Ye must be born again." Evidently mother was deeply impressed with the testimony and truth. She talked to me, however, very earnestly, endeavouring to show me the error of my ways. Finally, in order, if possible, to put me to shame, she made this happy hit: "Why, Samuel! Your talk is just like that of old Rachel Hull in Ireland. That's the very way she used to talk to me!" She thought that that would surely make me ashamed of my faith. But it had just the contrary effect. I at once saw the point, seized the undesigned testimony to the verity of Christian experience, and thanked God for the coincidence, that three thousand miles away I had found the same Saviour, and was happy in a like experience to that of a good old Methodist woman in the North of Ireland. I knew that in her heart mother had confidence in Mother Hull's piety. Instead, therefore, of being put to shame by the fact that I had been brought into the blessed experience of good old Mother Hull, I was greatly strengthened in the faith thereby. It was to me an additional evidence of the genuineness of vital, experimental Christianity.

During those early years of my Christian experience I had to contend not only earnestly but daily for the faith that was in me ; and especially did I have to defend and uphold the fact that we might be conscious of the love of God in Christ Jesus. My Roman Catholic friends ridiculed the idea of a person knowing their sins to be forgiven. Although their Church teaches that when the priest in the confessional stretching forth his right-hand towards the penitent, says " Our Lord Jesus Christ absolve thee, and I, by His authority, absolve thee from all thy sins, in the name of the Father, and of the Son and of the Holy Ghost. Amen."

" May the passion of our Lord Jesus Christ, the merits of the Blessed Virgin Mary, and of the saints, and whatsoever good thou shalt do, or whatsoever evil thou shalt suffer, be to thee unto the remission of thy sins, the increase of grace, and the recompense of everlasting life. Amen." Notwithstanding all this the sincere Roman worshipper has no assurance of pardon nor a personal consciousness of sins forgiven. He has no knowledge of the witness of the Spirit as taught by the Apostle Paul and as held out to be the privilege of every sincere believer in Christ : " For ye have not received the spirit of bondage again to fear ; but ye have received the Spirit of adoption, whereby we cry, Abba Father. The Spirit himself beareth witness with our spirit, that we are the children of God." And the repeated assurances throughout the Apostle John's writings that we do know that we are saved. Such as : " We know that we have passed from death unto life, because we love the brethren, etc."

In one of John Bunyan's books, the immortal dreamer

MOTHER HULL IN EVIDENCE. 91

of Bedford, I found the following passage which most aptly illustrates this idea of a conscious salvation, which characterizes Bible Christianity: "Upon a day the good providence of God did cast me to Bedford, to work on my calling (a tinker); and in one of the streets of that town, I came where there were three or four poor women sitting at a door in the sun, and talking about the things of God, and being now willing to hear them discourse I drew near to hear what they said, for I was now a brisk talker also myself in the matter of religion. But I may say *I heard, but I understood not;* for they were far above, out of my reach. Their talk was about a new birth, the work of God on their hearts, also how they were convinced of their miserable state by nature. They talked how God had visited their souls with His love in the Lord Jesus, and with what words and promises they had been refreshed, comforted, and supported against the temptations of the devil. Moreover they reasoned of the suggestions and temptations of Satan in particular; and told to each other by which they had been afflicted, and how they were borne up under his assaults. They also discoursed of their own wretchedness of heart, of their unbelief, and did contemn, slight, and abhor their own righteousness, as filthy and insufficient to do them any good. And methought they spake as if joy did make them speak; they spake with such pleasantness of Scripture language, and with such appearance of grace in all they said, that they were to me as if they had found a new world, as if they were people that dwelt alone, and were not to be reckoned amongst their neighbors."

As the Scriptures teach, "Out of the mouth of two or

three witnesses let every word be established," so I discover that my experience of the inner life, the new life in Christ, corresponds with that of those poor peasant women of England two hundred years ago, and that of Rachel Hull in the North of Ireland. And all are in harmony with the testimonies of prophet, psalmist, and Christian of the early centuries.

XVII

A PRIEST AT A METHODIST CLASS MEETING

ONE evening I was having a discussion with my brother, in regard to some of the points of difference between us. When we came to the doctrine of Purgatory and of having to pay for Masses for the relief of souls therein, he denied that the priests charged for such a service. I reminded him of what he might often have heard mother say in Ireland, " O that I had a few pounds to leave your ' Uncle Priest : (Rev. Samuel Young, her own brother) that he might pray for my poor soul after death." But he insisted that it was not so in this country. I told him that I would go to one of the priests and get the price list for him. As all the Irish priests in the city knew me, I was well aware it would be in vain to go to any one of them, so I went to the French priest whose church was on Ely Street. It was in the evening when I went. He had rooms in the rear of the church, where I found him, He received me very cordially, and I at once made known my errand. He supposed, of course, I was a good Catholic and had come to engage him to say Masses for the relief of some friend who had recently died. He told me the regular price for a " low " Mass was fifty cents, but for a " high " Mass, there was no stipulated price ; it all depended upon the circumstances of the applicant. It might be five or fifty or one hundred dollars, according to the ability to pay. I asked him the difference between the two kinds of Masses, "high" and "low." "There is no difference," he said, "in the prayers. They are exactly alike in both cases." "Why then," I asked him, "should the High Mass be so much more expensive ?" The reason given was this : "In a 'low' Mass the liturgy is simply read, the little boy serving Mass, responding ; and usually there is scarcely anyone present unless it may be an old woman or two. But when 'high' Mass is celebrated there is a large audience. The officiating priest intones the service. The choir, with the organ, respond, and as there are more people present to participate in the service and consequently more prayers are offered up, why of course the service is more efficacious and con sequently is worth more. If the prayers of one avail the prayers of many prevail more effectually."

Having learned from him all I wished to know in regard to the price of the Masses for the dead, we passed on to other subjects, and, ere long, he mistrusted that I was a Protestant. Then followed an interesting and spirited interview which lasted till a late hour. I found him bright, shrewd, and intelligent. I learned from him that evening that he was well informed in regard to Protestantism, especially the Protestant institutions of Rochester. That very day, he told me, he had visited the Rochester University, which had just been established by the Baptists. He went every Sunday night to some Protestant Church. He usually went, he said to the Brick Church to hear Dr. Shaw, who was then the most prominent and popular preacher in the city, or the Rev. A. C. George, pastor of the First Methodist Episcopal Church. He spoke especially of Mr. George's

PRIEST AT A METHODIST CLASS MEETING. 95

preaching. "I like to hear him," he said. "He is earnest, eloquent!" Just a few days before that he had attended a great Methodist Missionary Mass Meeting in Corinthian Hall when certain ministers were about going to California as missionaries, among whom was Rev. S. B. Rooney, a member of the Newark Conference, and now residing in Buffalo. In a word, I concluded that he knew more about the various churches and institutions of Protestantism in that city than possibly any one Protestant clergyman in it.

Seeing that he was so well informed on religious matters outside of his own church, I said to him, "Have you ever been to a Methodist Class Meeting?" "No, I have not," he replied. "Would you like to go?" I said to him. Upon his replying that he would, I arranged to take him with me to my class the following Wednesday evening.

I was then about eighteen years of age. I was in charge of the most interesting class in the Old First Church. In those days the class meeting was a live means of grace, a spiritual power in Methodism. The occasion for appointing one so young to such an important class as I then had charge of demands a word of explanation. The winter before, under the labors of the pastor, Rev. Mr. George, there had been a remarkable revival among the young people in the Sunday School, resulting in a large accession to the church. Of those who joined the church there were about thirty lads. These Mr. George placed in a class by themselves and put me in charge of them. The appointment, however, met with strong opposition from some of the older and more conservative members of the official board. They thought I was too young to be charged with such responsibilities and to thus become a member of the official board. However, I was appointed. Then in due time, the pastor saw the importance of the boys having the benefit of the experience of older Christians ; so he selected about an equal number of the more experienced members of the church, both men and women, and placed them in the class, thus making this class the best in the church.

When the time arrived, according to appointment, I met the priest, and he accompanied me to the church. The First Church was then situated on the corner of Fitzhugh and Buffalo Streets (now West Avenue) The class met in a room in the rear of the basement. As we passed through the large room, I asked him if he would like to speak in the meeting. He said, "No." There was about thirty present. It was a meeting of great spiritual interest. The testimonies given by old and young were edifying, the singing was hearty and spiritual, and the entire service was such as to make a favorable impression upon any unprejudiced mind. The priest paid the closest attention, and appeared to be deeply interested. I did not know what was working in his mind, but I conducted the class throughout with a view to his benefit. The meeting closed. We walked up the street together. Nothing was said in regard to the meeting. I asked him if he would like to visit the class again. He said he would, so I invited him to come the next week. As before, I went after him, and we went together again to class meeting. At the close of the meeting I asked him to speak. He accepted the invitation. He arose and commenced a labored address

PRIEST AT A METHODIST CLASS MEETING. 97

against Protestantism. I saw he was going to take too much time so I gave him a gentle hint which he readily took and soon closed his remarks. I made a brief reply which seemed to displease him very much. As soon as the meeting was closed he quickly left the church, and returned home alone.

During the interview I had with him, in explanation of his attending Protestant meetings, he told me that he had permission to do so from his bishop. I suppose he was a Jesuit spy, and being in charge of an obscure little church, he had plenty of time to go around and pick up items of intelligence in regard to the workings of the various institutions of Protestantism, which he reported to his superior in office.

Although I never visited him again nor had any conversation with him, yet I often saw him at the Sunday evening service when Dr. George was pastor. He always appeared as though he desired to conceal his identity, as he invariably carried an umbrella or cane and would sit with his chin resting on it.

XVIII.

CALLING AT A CONVENT

MY sister Eliza, who afterwards became a Sister of Charity and was connected with the Convent at Emmettsburgh, Md., was at this time identified with the Convent near St. Patrick's Cathedral, Rochester. Whenever we met at my father's or on the street, the subject of conversation always turned to religion. She was very earnest and importunate in her entreaties for me to return to the old faith. I at last told her that if she would find one passage in the Bible that authorized us to pray to the Virgin Mary or that in any way favored praying to her, I would at once renounce my present faith and return to the bosom of the Catholic Church. "O," said she, "that is the easiest thing imaginable." But when I pressed her to produce the passages, she said that she could not, as she was not sufficiently familiar with the Scriptures to do so, but if I would go down to the convent there was a Sister there who had been a Protestant for twenty-one years and she would readily do it for me. "All right," I said. The appointment was made, and I was to go down the following Tuesday.

When the day and hour arrived I put my little Bible in my pocket and started for the convent. I was ushered into the large waiting-room where I soon met my sister and the Sister of Charity who was a professed convert from Protestantism. I at once made known my errand. I told her that I did not come to have any controversy with her. All I wished was the scripture proof-texts

CALLING AT A CONVENT.

in support of worshipping the Blessed Virgin, and then I was prepared to return to the Catholic Church. "O," she said, "that will be a very easy matter." As she produced her Bible I pulled out of my pocket my little red-bound copy of the Word and laid it on the stand by my side. The sight of it seemed to unnerve her, and straightway losing her temper, she became very angry and said some very bitter things about my version of the Bible. "Do you call that a Bible?" she said. "That is no Bible. It is a book gotten up by Martin Luther, John Calvin, and John Wesley." "They were mighty smart men," said I, "if they got up such a book as this that I hold in my hand! But," I remarked, "never mind about my Bible, all I want to know is this, does your Bible authorize me to pray to the Virgin Mary?" She then quieted down and set about the task of finding the passages. In the back part of her Bible, as in many, if not all, the editions of the Douay Bible, there is a list of the distinctive doctrines of the Church with scripture proofs annexed. As I had been over the ground pretty thoroughly, I knew the first passage she would quote, 2 Cor. 1 11. She tried to find the passage but all in vain. She searched the Bible from Genesis to Malachi, but could not find Paul's Epistle to the Corinthians. I witnessed and secretly enjoyed her search. So after her knowledge of the Bible had been sufficiently tested and my patience sufficiently tried, I suggested to her that she would find it more readily by looking in the New Testament; which she did. But when she found it and read it, she was greatly chagrined, for the verse proved nothing of the kind. It is simply a request of the Apostle Paul that his

Corinthian brethren should pray for him: "Ye also helping together by prayer for us, that for the gift bestowed upon us by the means of many persons thanks may be given by many on our behalf." Not a single word about the Virgin Mary or the saints or angels praying for us is to be found in the passage. Well, as that was the strongest proof-text that she could produce, the prospect was not very bright for a convert that afternoon. When she saw that she was discomfited in her attempt to convince or convert me to the worship of Mary, through the Bible, she tried to win me over by personal appeal and earnest entreaty. The interview lasted about two hours. The conversation or controversy became very spirited and at times highly exciting and somewhat dramatic, my sister Eliza rushing across the room and begging me with tears not to talk so to the Sister. My only offence was that I got the start of her in argument, and put questions to her she could not answer. Instead of remaining on the defensive, I boldly assumed an aggressive attitude and pressed her sore on her own ground.

Having failed to furnish a single scripture text favoring prayers to the Virgin Mary or to any saint or angel, and being annoyed by certain proofs and arguments I presented against such worship, as a last resort they both came across the room to me, and getting down on their knees, entreated me to get down on mine and offer just one prayer to the Virgin, and they assured me if I would she would convert me right there. I replied, "Of course she would. For if I should kneel down and pray to her, it would be to acknowledge that I was already converted to her worship." So I stoutly resisted all their pleas and tears. I told them frankly I could not be caught in such a trap. Then when they saw that all their efforts were in vain, they desired me to go into the adjoining chapel and pray. I told them I would gladly do so. I was ready to pray anywhere. So I went in and knelt down and prayed to the Father in secret, while they, I suppose, supplicated the Virgin and the saints. Thus closed the most remarkable and memorable interview I ever had with a Roman Catholic.

The above narrative gives but a faint idea of the burning zeal and tireless devotion of that sister to win me back to what she honestly believed to be the true faith. Feeling as she did, she would have given her life to have rescued me from what she deemed a deadly apostasy. Such zeal and devotion furnishes a powerful lesson to every Protestant, enlightened by the Word of God. If Christian people were inspired with a like consecration to the work of saving the lost, the heathen would, ere long, be given to the Lord for His inheritance, and the uttermost parts of the earth for His possession.

My dear sister afterwards became a most devoted Sister of Charity. During the Civil War she nursed our sick and wounded soldiers in hospital and on the battlefield, in which service she contracted disease and died as the result of exposure and work near New Orleans where she had been sent to recover her health.

XIX.

THE PROFITS OF PURGATORY

WHILE the doctrines of the Roman Catholic Church are the same in all parts of the world, and the liturgy of the Mass is without variation, yet the discipline and customs of the Church vary in different countries and in different parts of the same country, according to the judgment or permission of the bishop in authority. In that part of Ireland in which I lived there were certain customs that prevailed, of which I have never heard in this country. Indeed, if they were practiced here, a scandal would be brought upon the Church. One of these customs was that of receiving offerings at funerals. The body being taken to the church, after the service was over, the clerk of the parish took his seat at a table within the chancel with paper, pen and ink. A plate was placed upon the lid of the coffin and the priest called upon all friends and relatives of the deceased to come forward and pay due respect to the memory of the departed by making a generous offering. As one after another came and placed his offering upon the plate, the priest announced the name and amount, making appropriate and appreciative comments on each gift and giver, the clerk in the meantime recording the same in the parish book. This was always regarded the most interesting, as it was the most profitable, part of the funeral service, especially to the officiating clergyman. The money, thus donated, went into the treasury of the church. The amount

THE PROFITS OF PURGATORY.

realized depended upon the wealth of the mourners and friends of the departed and the success of the priest in working upon the sympathies of those present.

The devices which the Roman Catholic Church adopts to secure money from its people, through Masses for the dead in Purgatory, are various and very successful.

While attending St. Mary's Church, Rochester, I was present one Sunday morning, when Father Carroll, the priest of the parish, adopted this plan by which to get money from his people : He organized a " Society for the relief of souls in Purgatory." He explained very fully the object of the organization and the great advantage to be gained by being a member of it. The design of the Society was to bring relief to the suffering souls in Purgatory through the prayers and suffrages of the faithful on earth. Each member, on joining the society, was to pay fifty cents, and that amount each following year, and in return they should have a Mass offered every month in the year for the relief of their friends in Purgatory. Father Carroll was very explicit in stating that it mattered not where or when their friends died ; the Masses would avail in their behalf. In urging upon his people the pious duty of affording relief to their suffering friends in the other world, he waxed exceedingly pathetic and eloquent, moving his parishioners to tears.

As the result of the appeal, hundreds united with the society. In the course of his remarks he showed his hearers the saving a membership would be to them. The price of a " low " Mass, then, was fifty cents, but under this arrangement they would secure twelve Masses for that sum.

When afterwards I learned that instead of each member of the society having a Mass offered for him or her each month, one Mass was said for the entire society, my faith was considerably shaken in the honesty of the plan. That, however, is in accordance with the teaching of the Church. The whole matter hinges on the *intention* of the officiating priest. If he *intends* the Mass for any number, it is just as efficacious as though he had offered one for each subject.

Although among intelligent Roman Catholics in America there is at times a strong feeling of protest, amounting in certain cases to indignation. at the greed of filthy lucre on the part of the hierarchy thus making merchandise of souls, yet it is rarely the case that a man has the courage of his convictions to speak out against such abuses. A case occurred recently in Buffalo, N. Y., which is worthy of special note. The Rev. George Zurcher, pastor of St. Joseph's Roman Catholic Church, delivered a sermon Nov. 5, 1899, in which he attacked the practice of collecting money for the special remembrance of souls in Purgatory in the Masses said on All Souls Day. He declared that the Masses were for the souls of those who had no friends on earth to pray for them. Father Zurcher said in his sermon:

"On the Sunday before All Souls' Day, in some churches, envelopes are distributed among the people. Every envelope contains a printed sheet of paper directing that the names of dead friends be written thereon, the whole list signed by the one who writes the names. It is customary to enclose a money offering in the envelope. On All Souls' Day the priest collects these envelopes with their contents. Now wherever the practice creates or gives the impression that the All Souls' Day Mass is said exclusively for those names collected in the envelopes, it is a fraud. I say it is a fraud because the All Souls' Day Mass which is written in every Mass Book on the altar of the Catholic Church for that day, is what its title and name says, a Mass for all the souls in Purgatory. And if a priest should wish to remember in the Mass of that day the soul of anyone in particular, or of such whose names are written on sheets of paper or for whom money is offered, it must be understood by the people that these souls should have a share in the Mass on that day, even if their names had not been collected by the priest. Should you ever attend Mass on All Souls' Day in a church where this fraud is practiced, denounce it. Let the envelope alone. Tell your friends to do the same."

Three days later Vicar General M. P. Connery, administrator of the diocese, who saw a report of Father Zurcher's sermon in print, wrote to him, charging that Father Zurcher had insulted the Church and subverted the truth. Father Connery demanded a denial that Father Zurcher had uttered the sermon, or that he should make a public retraction of it, under pain of suspension, and commanded him to appear before him. This Father Zurcher failed to do, but repeated his sermon and nailed the manuscript to the pulpit.

Since that time Father Zurcher has been suspended. He has appealed to the Archbishop Corrigan of New York City, but it is doubtful if he will secure any redress. In such a case the humble parish priest is under the heel of his Bishop, and it would be an exceptional case where a higher prelate would give heed to such an appeal.

The suspended priest is beloved by his people and held in the highest esteem by the non-Catholic citizens of Buffalo. He is, however, too independent and outspoken in regard to certain abuses in his church to suit many of his fellow-priests and communicants.

XX

THE NEW LIFE

AT the close of a period of fifty years' experience in the new life in Christ, I narrate the foregoing story of my conversion and a few of the many incidents connected therewith with the hope that good may be accomplished thereby. My aim has been to emphasize those distinctive truths of New Testament Christianity which form the pith and marrow of all genuine religion.

My conversion from Roman Catholicism was not a mere change of opinion or creed; it was the entrance into a new life. It was the dawn of a new day. In the simplicity and sincerity of my heart I sat at the feet of Jesus and learned of Him. And as I thus listened to His Divine voice I heard him say: "I thank Thee, O Father, Lord of heaven and earth, because Thou hast hid these things from the wise and prudent, and hast revealed them unto babes." I took heart and hope thereat and read and pondered the wonderful words of life with all the zest of an enthusiast. I followed closely the Gospel narrative. I discovered nothing obscure or mysterious in the words of Jesus. I read these words: "I am the Way, the Truth, and the Life; no man cometh unto the Father but by Me. I am the Door (into the way); by Me if any man enter in, he shall be saved, and shall go in and out and find pasture." I was like a child groping in the dark. I longed for the light. I was suffering from soul-hunger. Mine was the experience of the prodigal son, when he came to himself and said, "How many hired servants of my father's have bread enough and to spare, and I perish with hunger."

If there was aught in the absolution of the priest, and the worship of the Virgin, and the eating of the wafer that I did not receive, it was no fault of mine, for most sincerely, devoutly, and thoroughly did I conform to all the rules and regulations of the church. But it was all a mere form. There was no consciousness of relief, of rest, of restoration to the Divine favor. When I prayed to Mary I had no evidence that she heard me, for there is no warrant for her worship from the mouth of Jesus or His Apostles. And when the priest placed the wafer on my tongue and assured me that I then received the Lord Jesus Christ in the entirety of His nature, human and divine, surely I ought to have experienced a wonderful change. But I did not, though I was a devout communicant.

It was at this point where the new life in Christ bore a strong contrast to the old life of forms and ceremonies and sacraments. I proved by experience that the letter killeth but the Spirit giveth life. The law of the Spirit of life in Christ Jesus had made me free from the law of sin and death, and I had an experience of the glorious liberty of a child of God. I had been seeking for goodly pearls, when, lo ! I found one pearl of great price. I had such a keen sense of hunger that no semblance or symbol of food would satisfy, nothing but the Divine Reality. That, I found in Him who said, " I am the living Bread which came down from heaven ; if any man eat of this bread he shall live forever ; and the bread that I will give is my flesh, which I shall give for the life of the world. For my flesh is meat indeed,

THE NEW LIFE. 109

and my blood is drink indeed." In that same wonderful discourse, found in the sixth chapter of John's Gospel, Jesus tells us how we may become partakers of His Divine nature. It is by coming to Him and believing on Him. "I am the bread of life," said Jesus, " he that cometh to Me shall never hunger ; and he that believeth on Me shall never thirst." And again, lest His disciples or any after them should stumble over His profound words, He said : " It is the Spirit that quickeneth ; the flesh profiteth nothing : the words that I speak unto you, they are spirit and they are life."

As the centre of Roman Catholic worship is in the assumed miracle of transubstantiation, wherein it is claimed the real presence of Christ is in the sacrament ; so, likewise, the life, the mystery, the power of the Gospel lies in this divine verity : " CHRIST IN YOU, THE HOPE OF GLORY." " *If a man love me,*" said Jesus, "*he will keep my words ; and my Father will love him, and we will come unto Him, and make our abode with Him.*" That is the REAL PRESENCE in which the Bible Christian believes, and which is the privilege of every true believer to enjoy. In the faith and experience of this vital truth all evangelical Protestants unite. Here we are one. There may be variations as to church polity and doctrinal views, but touching Christian experience, the life of faith, we see eye to eye, so that we can unite in the Apostolic Creed : " There is one body, and one Spirit, even as ye are called in one hope of your calling ; one Lord, one faith, one baptism, one God and Father of all, who is above all, and through all, and in you all."

During all these years of my Christian experience and ministry, I have been upborne and inspired by a consciousness of the Divine presence. The words of Jesus have been of solid comfort: "He that loveth Me shall be loved of My Father, and I will love him, and will manifest myself to him." I could testify also with Paul that the Gospel of Christ is the power of God unto salvation to every one that believeth; and I was thus enabled to realize the force of the Apostle's testimony: "It pleased God to reveal His Son in me."

> "What we have felt and seen,
> With confidence we tell;
> And publish to the sons of men
> The signs infallible.
>
> We who in Christ believe
> That He for us hath died:
> We all His unknown peace receive,
> And feel His blood applied."

XXI.

THE IMMACULATE CONCEPTION OF THE VIRGIN MARY

ON December 8th, 1854, Pius IX., with a tremulous voice, delivered in Latin the following decree :—

"*We declare, pronounce, and define that the doctrine which holds that the Blessed Virgin Mary, at the first instant of her conception, by a singular privilege and grace of the Omnipotent God, the Saviour of Mankind, was preserved immaculate from all stain of original sin, has been revealed by God, and therefore should firmly and constantly be believed by the faithful.*"

The cannon of the castle of St. Angelo, the joyful chime of all the bells of Rome, the enthusiastic plaudits of the assembled thousands, the magnificent illumination of St. Peter's Church, and the splendour of the most gorgeous festive rites, gave response to the infallible decree. It was a grand pageant, befitting an idolatrous enthusiasm.

The pope himself, with " trembling joy," crowned the image of the Virgin ; medals of Austrian gold were struck, and distributed in her honour ; " Rome," say the beholders, " was intoxicated with joy." An infallible voice had spoken ; a new article of faith was announced by " divine " authority ; the people rejoiced in hope that Mary would be yet more " Propitious," that her " prevalent " intercession would give peace and plenty, would stay the power of infidelity, put an

112 FROM ROME TO CHRIST.

end to insurrection, and crown Rome with higher honours and success. The controversy of seven hundred years is brought to a final decision ; Rome is committed irrevocably to the Virgin mother, conceived without original sin. Doubt now is heresy.

ORIGIN AND GROWTH OF THE DOGMA.

In the first place the stoutest defenders of the doctrine do not pretend that it has any support from the Bible. The false doctrines of the Roman Church have all a uniform groundwork. Their root is a certain kind of piety, which, however, is not regulated according to the rule of the Word of God. But as soon as such proceedings have obtained a measure of authority by force of custom, speculation steps forward and spiritualizes them into a theory. "So long as the new doctrine fights its battles from the outside, its progress is slow ; but once in possession of the centre, the Papal chair, it wins one battle after another, and in the end lays its yoke upon the necks of all who are under the dominion of Rome."

There is scarcely a single Romish dogma that furnishes so clear an illustration of this manner of growth as this one we are now considering. The first historic germ of this colossal error we discover in the city of Lyons when a few pious devotees, in self-imposed devotion, celebrate as a festival the conception of Mary—not the immaculate conception, but simply the conception of Mary. Then as early as the middle of the fourth century, the unbridled imagination of one Ephraem, a Syrian Christian, overstepped the bounds, and he praised the Virgin in a manner which departed widely from the model of the pure doctrine. He calls her, Most Holy Lady, the pre-eminently pure one both in soul and body, that she is a complete dwelling-place of the full grace of the Holy Spirit. He praises her as occupying a position next to the Godhead, as a light which enlightens the souls of believers, yea, even as the atonement of sinners. Now the waters of imaginative praise, overflowed the church in streams. Accordingly, John of Damascus, about the year 720, not only called her the common Salvation of the whole world, but also asserted without hesitation, that prayer must be made to her throughout all eternity. Such extravagant and unscriptural expressions were not confined, however, to the fervid East. One of the noted doctors of the church, a friend of Hildebrand, calls her the "Queen of the World, the Star of the Sea, his mediator with God the Father, and the means of our new birth." He even declares that "all power is given to her in heaven and in earth, and that to her nothing was absolutely impossible; for she, who has expiated our sins, stands before God as mistress, not as maid."

About this time they not only invented stories and wrote poems about Mary, but even honoured her as their goddess. They used to offer her small cakes; they held meetings in her honour, and conferred titles upon her. In particular, at a certain solemn time in the year, they used to dress up a four-cornered stool, spread it over with linen, put their small cakes upon it, and having offered them in the name of Mary, they used to eat them. They made their ideal for themselves, and then worshipped it! Thus people began, very soon in the East, and one hundred and fifty years later in the West, to pray to her openly. Indeed, in 787 such prayers became law for a great part of the church, in consequence of the decisions of the second Synod of Nicea.

The worship of Mary was greatly encouraged, about this time, by the multiplication of the festivals in her honour. Thus the death of Mary the Virgin imperceptibly passed into her assumption to heaven, while her birth suggested to those who celebrated it the privilege of absolute purity. Thus the Western Church had, as early as the year 1100, removed far from the precepts of the Word of God, in her view of the mother of our Lord.

We now reach an important epoch in the evolution of Mariolatry. It was in the city of Lyons that we first witnessed the rise of this species of idolatry. It is now in the same city we witness in the church of St. John the Baptist, the celebration, for the first time, the conception of Mary—not the immaculate conception, but simply the conception of Mary. That was on the 8th of December, 1139. This innovation came by the same by-path, in following which the arbitrary and undisciplined devotion of the church of the middle ages departed ever more and more widely from the guidance of the Word of God. Thus it is that each novelty, unlikely as it may have appeared, has become a root of bitterness, which has overrun, with its luxuriant shoots, and partly choked, the good seed of the kingdom. But God would not leave His people to fall into these snares without a warning. Consequently, at this time, God moved the man who should be the witness against it, a man whose voice at that time prevailed more than that of the pope himself. Bernard, Abbot of Clair Vaux, one of the most saintly men of that age, and one of the most gifted, was God's voice against this new error. He wrote the canons of St. John an energetic letter, wherein he censures their unbridled devotion, and warns them in the name of their forefathers. Mark you, at this time, near the middle of the 12th century, the doctrine of the "immaculate" conception had not been mooted or advanced,—just simply her conception. In writing against having festivals in honour of Mary this great Father and Saint of the church says :—" Why, if desired, we might upon the same grounds appoint special festivals to the honour of both the parents of Mary, and any one who wished it could demand them in like manner for their grand-parents and great-grandparents, and so on without end—festivals without number." I will give another passage from the writings of this noted father of the church, showing how strongly he was opposed to that doctrine which is now the pet dogma of the church. Says he, "A solemn feast always involves the idea that the thing celebrated is holy. Is such the case with the celebration of the Virgin ? He who maintains that must yield to the belief that Mary had been sanctified before she had existed Or can a new holiness have forced itself into the midst of the union of Joachim and Anna ? But those who are not satisfied with this explanation will be obliged to admit that Mary, like the God-man, was conceived of the Holy Ghost Himself, without the co-operation of a man. *All that is manifestly false.* Jesus Christ alone had the prerogative of immaculate conception ; every other, even the Virgin Mary herself, must confess, ' Lo, I am shapen in iniquity, and in sin did my mother conceive me.'" "So then," says Bernard, "the holy Virgin would willingly dispense with such false honours. An innovation, such as this, is the mother of confusion, the sister of superstition, and the daughter of levity." Soon, however, after the death of Bernard, an English Abbot, Nocholas of St. Albans, started up and opposed these arguments that had been advanced, and so ably sustained, and anon, the innovation spreads from cloister to cloister; and the year 1300 witnesses already two-thirds of the clergy of England, and one-third of that of France, amongst its adherents.

The most noted champion of the new dogma at this time was Duns Scotus (John Duns), the Franciscan, the most gifted of the scholastics of his day. There was at one time a great contention between the Dominicans and Franciscans at Paris, respecting the immaculate conception. In order to satisfy both parties, the pope had allowed a solemn discussion to be held there. A vast multitude of doctors were assembled on the side of the Dominicans; but for the honour of Mary, Scotus was chosen in her defence. When Scotus was about to commence his discussion, in favour of the immaculate conception, he observed a picture of Mary hanging in the hall where he and his opponents were assembled for the debate, and he humbly implored her help. As a sign that she heard and answered his prayer, the picture, it is said, bowed its head, and remained ever afterwards in that position. This absurd story was often repeated by the Spanish in the 17th century, during the contentions over the immaculate conception. Lucas Wadding, the historian, does not hesitate to record it in his annals, as having been firmly believed.

THE IMMACULATE CONCEPTION. 117

Scotus won a great victory in the debate which brought to his side the University of Paris, which before this had been an opponent of the dogma, and now becomes one of its most zealous friends.

The doctrine of the Immaculate Conception is at once confronted with several difficulties. It is not supported by any evidence of Holy Scripture ; it is a comparative novelty in theology ; and it is distinctly opposed to the doctrine of original sin.

As to Scripture evidence, only two passages are adduced by the defenders of this doctrine. The first is Gen. iii. 15—" I will put enmity between thee and the woman, and between thy seed and her seed ; it shall bruise thy head, and thou shalt bruise his heel." As there is absolutely no ground whatever for using it in such a sense, it is only so used to meet the necessity of finding a feigned scriptural support for the doctrine. The other passage alleged is the salutation of the angel, Luke i 28, 30, 42, coupled with the words spoken by Elizabeth—" Hail, thou art highly favoured, the Lord is with thee : blessed art thou among women. . . . Fear not, Mary, for thou hast found favour with God. . . . Blessed art thou among women, and blessed is the fruit of thy womb." But why these words should be so interpreted those who use them for the purpose do not say. They are, in fact, uncritically and illogically forced into the service of the doctrine.

That the dogma of the Immaculate Conception is a comparative novelty in theology is historically certain. In evidence that the post-apostolic fathers never dreamed of such a vagary, we mention the names of the following leading divines of the church in the early centuries :—Ireneus, Tertullian, Origen, Basil the Great, and Chrysostom, who do not hesitate to speak of faults of Mary, of her being rebuked by Christ. Chrysostom ascribes to her " excessive ambition " at the marriage festival at Cana. Basil thinks that she, too, " wavered at the time of the crucifixon." All of which statements are utterly inconsistent, not only with the dogma of the " immaculate conception," but also with a belief in her perfect innocency.

Lastly, this doctrine is distinctly opposed to that of original sin. The Word of God is express and unmistakeable as to the fact that *all* are conceived in sin. There is not one particle of evidence that the conception of the Virgin Mary, by her mother, differed in any respect from that of other children by other men.

The definition of such a dogma presupposes a divine revelation ; for God omniscient alone knows the fact of the immaculate conception, and as the Bible nowhere informs us of it, God must have revealed it to Pius the Ninth in 1854, either directly, or through the voice of the six hundred bishops assenting to his view. *But if he was really infallible he did not need the advice of others.*

Since the infallibility of the Pope has been declared, and the Immaculate Conception decreed a dogma of the Church to which all must subscribe under penalty of damnation, the matter of papal infallibility has been placed in a serious dilemma. The decree of Pius Ninth is in opposition to the express declarations of preceding pontiffs ; pope is arrayed against pope ; infallibility is discordant with infallibility. Peter's chair is divided against itself. And how, then, can that Kingdom stand ? One of their own noted authors has collected together the opinions of *seven* popes that are adverse to, or irreconcilable with the dogma.

"Thus the papacy, in committing itself to this new and idolatrous dogma, is in hostility to Scripture, to universal consent, and also to itself. It explains the sense of scripture by tradition, and it explains the sense of tradition by an infallible expositor, and that infallible expositor contradicts himself. The new dogma makes *the whole of the early church to* have been ignorant of a truth which is now declared to be necessary to the faith. It makes Innocent III. Innocent V., and Clement V., to have taught heresy ; it puts the greatest scholastic divines under the ban ; and, while doing this, it declares that what is now decreed has always been of the faith of the Church, and that it is a part of the revelation of God, given through Christ and the apostles, and handed down by constant succession and general consent."

We have brought this doctrine forward into the light of historic investigation, not merely because it is the newest fruit of the papacy, but more especially because it can be shown more clearly as to this one than as to any other, how unapostolical, how modern, this system is, which gives itself out as apostolic and old. When I was a Catholic did not believe this doctrine under consideration. I was not obliged to believe it. It was not then one of the tenets of the church. But if after the year 1870, at which time the Vatican Council endorsed the decision of the Pope, I had wished to return to the church I could not have done so unless I had subscribed thereto. Or if I had been a member in good standing in the church up to 1870 and then declined accepting the new dogma I should have been liable to excommunication, and in danger of the damnation of hell. Some of the most distinguished scholars and saintly men in the Roman church were excommunicated because they held out against submitting to the new decree. God is represented by the prophet Malachi as saying, "I am the Lord, I change not" (Mal. iii. 6). The Church of Rome cannot say that, for from time immemorial she has been changing her creed, and these changes have been made at the expense of the peace and unity of the Church.

We see from the story of this new dogma how the Papacy by giving its solemn sanction has severed itself from tradition and the Bible, and in their stead has professedly accepted public opinion for its basis, and thus has gone back on its own rule of faith, *viz.* : *Tradition and the Holy Scriptures.*

Thus the Bull of the 8th of December, 1854, is practically a rupture of the Papacy with its own past. A rupture with the principles to which the Council of Trent clung with the tenacity of a drowning man. As the dogma of the "Immaculate Conception" is one of the chief characteristic features of Modern Romanism, it widens the breach between it and Bible Christianity.

XXII.

DOES THE PAPACY ENDORSE OR AUTHORISE THE MURDER OF HERETICS ?

THE recent publication of Lord Acton's letters to Mary Gladstone, daughter of the late distinguished British Premier, has created a genuine sensation among the Romish hierarchy. Who was Lord Acton ? He was the greatest scholar and the most noted Roman Catholic layman of his day. He lived and died in the Roman church. He was a British Peer, a member of the House of Lords, a Professor of History in Cambridge University. He was a prodigy of learning, a walking cyclopedia. He was a life-long friend of Gladstone, and for many years he maintained a correspondence with the Premier's gifted daughter.

Although he never broke with the Church, yet he had no use for the Papacy nor the Jesuits who controlled it, being so well versed in the history of both. He and Professor Dollinger of Munich, the great German Catholic scholar, who was excommunicated by Pope Pius IX., were bosom friends. Lord Acton went to Rome during the session of the Vatican Council, 1870, and did his utmost, by pen, and persuasive speech with the members of the Council and those outside to prevent the Council from proclaiming the dogma of Papal Infallibility. That Acton was not excommunicated as well as Dollinger was because he was a layman and in view of his high standing before the British public as a great scholar, and his marked personal influence. When these letters were written to Mary Gladstone—now Mrs. Drew—it was not expected that they would ever be published, a fact which gives the extracts we take from them the greater weight. As early as 1898, before Lord Acton's death, there was a demand for the publication of the letters, and the author, with certain reservations, gave his assent. The letters embrace a wide range of thought. They touch upon current events, of vital importance, political and religious. The importance and value of the opinions and historic facts pertaining to the Papacy and Jesuitism, are enhanced by the fact that the author was one of the most distinguished historical scholars of his day, and while a true Catholic he was not blind to the blighting influence of Jesuitism and the Papacy.

The following extracts are from a recent work published by McMillan & Co., of London, entitled "The Letters of Lord Acton to Mary Gladstone."

In the *London Times* of November 9th and 24th, 1874, Lord Acton said : " The *Corpus juris* makes the murder of Protestants lawful. Pope Pius the Fifth justified the assassination of Elizabeth. Pope Gregory the Thirteenth condoned, or rather applauded, the massacre of Saint Bartholomew."

" A speculative Jesuitism separate from theories of tryanny, mendacity, and murder, keeping honestly clear of the Jesuit with his lies, of the Diminican with his fagots, of the Popes with their massacres, has not yet been brought to light.'

" Cardinal Newman defended the Syllabus, and the Syllabus justified all those atrocities. Pope Pius the Fifth held that it was sound Catholic doctrine that any man may stab a heretic condemned by Rome, and that every man is a heretic who attacks the papal prerogatives. Borromeo wrote a letter for the purpose of causing a few Protestants to be murdered."

"The Irish massacre was more appalling to the imagination than the Sepoy rebellion, because it was nearer and of vaster proportions. A respectable writer who lived in Ireland believes that there were 300,000 victims."

The clearest statement of his own opinion upon Jesuitism and the Jesuits is found in a private letter to Premier Gladstone Among other things Lord Acton says · " Putting aside the ignorant mass, and those who are incapable of reasoning, I do not know of a religious and educated Catholic who really believes that the See of Rome is a safe guide to salvation. . . . In short, I do not believe there are Catholics who, sincerely and intelligently, believe that Rome is right, and that Dollinger is wrong. And therefore I think you are too hard on Jesuits, or too gentle with Jesuitism. You say, for instance, that it—Jesuitism —promotes untruthfulness. I don't think that is fair. It not only promotes, it inculcates, distinct mendacity and deceitfulness. In certain cases it is made a duty to lie. But those who teach this doctrine do not become habitual liars in other things."

" An account of Catholicism which assumes that, in the middle of the 17th century, Rome had not commenced to burn (Protestants), is an account which studiously avoids the real and tragic issues of the time. The part of Hamlet is omitted, by design. . . . Familiar instances must have been remembered, as they had read in the most famous theological treatise of the last generation by what gradation of torments a Protestant ought to die. They knew that whoever obstructed the execution of that law forfeited his life, that the murder of a heretic was not only permitted but rewarded, that it was a virtuous deed to slaughter Protestant men and women, until they were all exterminated.

" To keep these abominations out of sight is the same offence as to describe the Revolution (French) without the guillotine.

" There was no mystery about these practices, no scruple, and no concealment. Although never repudiated, and although retrospectively sanctioned by the Pope in his Syllabus, they fell into desuetude, under pressure from France, and from Protestant Europe. But they were defended, more or less boldly, down to the peace of Westphalia (1648). The most famous Jesuits countenanced them, and were bound to countenance them, for the papacy had.

" The inquisition is peculiarly the weapon, and peculiarly the work of the Popes. It stands out from all those things in which they co-operated, followed, or assented as the distinctive features of papal Rome.

" It was set up, renewed, and perfected by a long series of acts emanating from the supreme authority in the Church. No other institution, no doctrine, no ceremony, is so distinctly the individual creation of the papacy, except the Dispensing power. It—the inquisition—is the principal thing with which the papacy is identified, and by which it must be judged.

"The principle of the Inquisition is the Pope's sovereign power over life and death. Whosoever disobeys him should be *tried* and *tortured* and *burnt*; If that cannot be done, formalities may be dispensed with, and the *culprit may be killed like an outlaw.*

"That is to say the principle of the Inquisition is murderous, and a man's opinion of the papacy is regulated and determined by his opinion about *religious assassination.*

"If he honestly looks upon it as an abomination, he can only accept the Primacy with a drawback, with precaution, suspicion, and aversion for its acts. If he accepts the Primacy with confidence, admiration, unconditional obedience, *he must have made terms with murder.*

"Therefore the most awful imputation in the catalogue of crimes rests, according to the measure of their knowledge and their zeal, upon those whom we call Ultramontanes (Jesuits). The controversy, primarily, is not about probelms of theology ; it is about the spiritual state of man's soul, who is the defender, the promoter, the accomplice of murder. Every limitation of papal credit and authority which effectually disassociates it from the reproach, which breaks off its solidarity with assassins and washes away the guilt of blood, will solve most other problems. At least, it is enough for my present purpose to say, *that blot is so large and foul that it precedes and eclipses the rest, and claims the first attention.*

" I will show you what Ultramontanism (the Papacy) makes of good men, by an example very near home. Saint Charles Borromeo, when he was the Pope's nephew and minister, wrote a letter requiring Protestants to be murdered, and complaining that no heretical heads were forwarded to Rome, in spite of the reward that was offered for them. His editor, with perfect consistency, publishes the letter with a note of approval. Cardinal Manning not only holds up to the general veneration of mankind the authority that canonized this murderer, but makes him in a special manner his own patron, joins the Congregation of Oblates of St. Charles, and devotes himself to the study of his acts and the propagation of his renown."

Lord Acton contributed to the *North British Review* a learned essay on the Massacre of Saint Bartholomew, in which he marshalled the facts, in a masterly manner, in favor of the theory that the *murder of the Huguenots had been pre-meditated at Rome.*

Sir John went to Rome some time before the opening of the Vatican Council of 1870, full of interest in the result, and full of sympathy with the distinguished minority who were prepared to resist the forging of fresh chains upon their freedom. He wrote frequent reports of the Council and its proceedings, chiefly to Mr Gladstone and Professor Dollinger. In writing of the action of the Council in requiring submission to Papal decrees on matters not articles of faith, he says :—" They were confirming without let or question, a power they saw in daily exercise ; they were investing with new authority the existing Bulls, and giving unqualified sanction to the inquisitor and the Index, to *the murder of heretics and the deposing of kings.* They approved what they were called to reform, and blessed with their lips what their hearts knew to be accursed."

At the very opening of the Council, regulations were issued which gave the Pope the sole right of making decrees and defining dogmas. "The sole legislative authority," Lord Acton wrote, " has been abandoned to the Pope. We have to meet an *organized conspiracy to establish a power which would be the most formidable enemy of liberty, as well as science in the world.*" "*Catholics,*" he declared, "*would at once become iredeemable enemies of civil and religious liberty.* They would have to profess a false system of morality, and to repudiate literary and scientific sincerity. *They would be as dangerous to civil society in the school as in the State.*"

A STRIKING AND STARTLING TESTIMONY FROM A GREAT ROMAN CATHOLIC SCHOLAR.

Professor Ignaz Von Dollinger was one of the most distinguished scholars of the Roman Church. For forty-seven years he had been an active professor of theology in one of the great Universities of Germany. Because he would not subscribe to the new dogmas decreed by the Pope and the Vatican Council, he was excommunicated. In writing to the Pope's Nuncio in regard to the judgment pronounced against him, he says :—" During this long period—forty-seven years—I always taught the contrary of what was decided by Pius IX. in 1870. The whole world knew or might have known what I believed and taught on this question. I taught what I had learned from my masters, what had been confirmed by my researches, and what I found in the historical and theological works which I judged to be the most reliable, namely, that the infallibility of the Pope was an opinion that had appeared at a very late period, but which was now tolerated in the church."

The following extract from this letter is significant and important, proving from this high authority that the Church of Rome approves of and authorizes the murder of heretics or Protestants when it is for the good of the Church. Professor Dollinger says :—" I take the liberty of citing a characteristic fact. When the Archbishop, according to his own words, obeying the orders of the Pope, communicated to me the sentence that had been pronounced against me, he informed me that I had incurred all the punishments which are heaped by the canonical law upon those who are excommunicated. The first and most important of these punishments is contained in the celebrated Bull of Pope Urban II., which decides that *every one may put to death one who is excommunicated, when it is done from a motive of zeal for the Church!* At the same time he had sermons preached against me from all the pulpits of Munich, and the effect produced by these declamations was such that the Chief of the Police informed me that attacks were being plotted against me, and that I should do well not to go out without company."

Professor Dollinger, in writing to Pastor Widman, who had written to him for counsel, in speaking of the hopeless condition in which affairs are in in Rome, says :—
" In the whole of this Papal community, within and without the confines of Italy, there is no longer any moving power but one, in the presence of which all others,

PAPACY AND THE MURDER OF HERETICS. 129

the episcopacy, the cardinalate, the spiritual orders, the schools, etc., remain passive—and that is the Order of the Jesuits. It is the soul and sovereign of the whole of the Roman Church. . . . *The Jesuits are the incarnation of superstition united with despotism. To rule mankind by means of the Pope, who has become subservient to them—this is their task, their aim, and their art, which they practice in a masterly way.* Hence their endeavours to make religion mechanical, *the sacrifice of the intellect*, which they highly recommend, the training of souls to unconditioned and blind obedience, etc."

Professor Dollinger regards the adoption, by Rome, of Liguori's works as the principal text-book on morals for the priesthood, as the greatest monstrosity that has ever occurred in the domain of theological doctrine. He says Liguori was " a man whose false morals, perverse worship of the Virgin Mary, constant use of the grossest fables and forgeries, make his writings a store—house of errors and lies. In the whole range of Church history, I do not know a single example of such a terrible and such a pernicious confusion."

XXIII.

ROME AND SIN

THE Romish doctrine in regard to sin is on the whole the most dangerous, deceptive, and deleterious of any of the dogmas propagated by that church. It is not in harmony with the teachings of Holy Scripture respecting sin, nor is it in its practical working conducive to the highest state of morals. It encourages a degree of laxity in certain lines of moral conduct that militates against the upbuilding of a Christian character after the pattern of Jesus Christ in the New Testament. Rome teaches that there are two kinds of sin—*mortal* and *venial*. The former is deadly and exposes the soul to eternal punishment, the latter is of trifling moment, such as little deceptions, fibs, idle, foolish words, petty thefts, etc., etc. Such sins need not be confessed to the priest, as they only subject one who dies in that state to the fires of purgatory. The doctors of the church, however, have always been sorely puzzled concerning the dividing line between the two kinds of sin. And well they may be, for being of the same nature, and both springing from the same root they are kith and kin.

There is a passage in Baroness Von Zedtwitz's new book, "The Double Doctrine of the Church of Rome,"[*] relevant to this subject, and worthy of being quoted. (The "Baroness," before her marriage, was Miss Caldwell, of Philadelphia, Pa., who founded the Roman Catholic University of Washington, D.C. In view of her wealth, literary culture, and high social position she was

---

[*] Fleming H. Revell Co., New York, London, and Edinburgh.

brought into close contact with the Roman prelacy in America and Catholic countries of Europe. Even in America in her "early girlhood" she had serious misgivings in regard to the "Unchristian conduct of almost all the prelates with whom she came in contact," but "never ceased to hope and believe that when womanhood had ripened her judgment, those apparent inconsistences would be fully explained." But when she came to travel abroad in Catholic countries, especially the seat and centre of Roman power, her eyes were fully opened to the "true inwardness" of the papacy. She says, "Romanism, to be understood, must be traced to its source, and it is to the College of Cardinals in Rome, and the 'Propaganda,' one must look for the true confirmation of its spirit." " Revolt," she says, " was the inevitable result of my search for enlightenment, and I struggled to be free ; but from the desert waste of Esoteric Catholicism but few can find the true path back to Christianity, and mine was a long and dreary search." Finally, after a patient, persistent, prayerful sincere search after the truth, she records this decision :—" *In the name of Christ, whose pure image had been long blurred by dross of Popery, in the name of Righteousness and Duty, I cast from me what was left of the garb of Romanism, and resolved to stand before my God, as an upright, if an unclothed soul.*")

The following is the quotation referred to :—" The standard of veracity in the Church of Rome differs seriously from that used by moralists in general. The principal and most influential guide upon questions of morals, in the Roman Catholic Church, is always Alphonsus de Liguori, who is not only a saint of the Church (since

1836), and declared by the fact of his canonization to be perfectly sound in all his doctrine, but is also a ' Doctor ' of the same Church (since 1871), which means that he is one whose teaching deserves to be accepted and followed by everyone. His work on Moral Theology is accordingly the standard now in use, and the others currently employed adopt its principles. Here is what he lays down on the subject of speaking the truth. "*Every kind of equivocation or quibbling which comes short of direct lying but is intended to deceive the hearer, and does in fact deceive him, is always lawful for ' a just cause.'* " An example of each kind will help to make the matter plainer. A man asked if a particluar thing be true, which he knows to be true, but does not wish to admit, may lawfully reply : " I say, No," meaning thereby only, " I utter the word, No," and not, " I declare the thing did not happen." This and many others of a similar character are put by Liguori himself (Theol. Mor., IV. : 151-167).

On turning to the words of Jesus in the Gospel we find a very different interpretation of those sins that the Roman Church calls *venial*.

Says Jesus : " Let your communication be, Yea, yea ; Nay, nay : for whatsoever is more than these cometh of evil." " I say unto you, That every idle word that men shall speak, they shall give account thereof in the day of judgment, For by thy words thou shalt be justified, and by thy words thou shalt be condemned."

And Saint Paul gives expression to some very plain truths to certain Christians to whom he wrote concerning those sins that Romanists count *venial*. Says

ROME AND SIN.

he: "Wherefore putting away lying, speak every man truth with his neighbour. Let no corrupt communication proceed out of your mouth, but that which is good to the use of edifying, that it may minister grace unto the hearers. Nor foolish talking, nor jesting, which are not convenient." Place this bugle-blast of Paul in the interest of sincerity and truth against the deceptive Romish casuistry of Liguori: "Therefore seeing we have this ministry, as we have received mercy we faint not, but have renounced the hidden things of dishonesty. not walking in craftiness, nor handling the word of God deceitfully, but by manifestation of the *truth* commending ourselves to every man's conscience in the sight of God."

Innumerable quotations and illustrations from the Bible might be given to show that the Romish idea of sin has no foundation in the Word of God. The heart is the seat of all sin. "Out of the heart," says Jesus, "proceed evil thoughts." "He that committeth sin," says the Apostle John, "is of the devil." Sin is the transgression of the law. All unrighteousness is sin. And the Holy Spirit has come into the world to convict of sin. All sin is of the devil.

XXIV.

THE FORGIVENESS OF SIN—SCRIPTURAL AND ROMAN

THE teaching of the Holy Scriptures in regard to the forgiveness of sin through the infinite mercy of God, and the atoning death of Christ, is most explicit and clear, and full of comfort. "Come now, and let us reason together, saith the Lord; though your sins be as scarlet, they shall be as white as snow; though they be red like crimson, they shall be as wool"—Isaiah i. 18. "Let the wicked forsake his way, and the unrighteous man his thoughts: and let him return unto the Lord, and He will have mercy upon him; and to our God, for He will abundantly pardon"—Isaiah lv. 7. "I will forgive their iniquity, and I will remember their sin no more"—Jer. xxxi. 34. "I, even I, am He that blotteth out thy transgressions for Mine own sake, and will not remember thy sins"—Isaiah xliii. 25. "He will subdue our iniquities; and Thou wilt cast all their sins into the depth of the sea"—Mic. vii. 19. "As far as the east is from the west, so far hath He removed our transgressions from us."—Ps. ciii. 12. Those passages are from the Old Testament, and their number might be multiplied.

We come to the New Testament, and from the lips of Jesus as He went about doing good, forgiving sin, healing the sick, comforting the sorrowing, to the last utterance of the inspired record from the pen of the beloved disciple John, we hear nothing but the exultant note of joy and thanksgiving over sins pardoned through the power and blood of the Son of God. We hear nothing of " doing penance " to make amends for the wrong done ; nothing of works or deeds of merit. It is all of free grace. As Paul expresses it : " Not by works of righteousness which we have done, but according to His mercy He saved us, by the washing of regeneration and the renewing of the Holy Ghost ; which He shed on us abundantly through Jesus Christ our Saviour."

When Jesus forgave a man his sins, He imposed no penance, but gave him His blessing, and told him to go and sin no more. When on the day of Pentecost Peter preached to those who, by cruel hands, had crucified the Lord of life, and as they were pricked in their heart and said to Peter and the rest, " Men and brethren, what shall we do ? " Peter said unto them, " Repent and be baptized, every one of you, in the name of Jesus Christ, for the remission of sins." Think of Peter and the eleven apostles on the day of Pentecost, hearing the confessions of the three thousand converts on that day, granting absolution, and then assigning to each one a given amount of penance in order that they might make satisfaction to God for all the wrong they had done Such an idea is preposterous, and is as foreign to the Spirit and genius of the Gospel as day is from night. And so all through the history of the Acts of the Apostles, in the founding of the primitive church, we find no trace of priestly absolution or the sacrament of penance. All of that came in after years. The distinctive doctrinal system, and ecclesiastical polity of the Church of Rome has a two-fold object : *Holding the laity under the power of the priesthood, and enriching the treasury of the church.*

In the confessional the penitent is taught to believe that the priest has absolute power to forgive sins. Here are a few quotations from the Catechism of the Council of Trent :—" Our sins are forgiven by the absolution of the priest." " The voice of the priest, who is legitimately constituted a minister for the remission of sins, is to be heard as that of Christ Himself. " The absolution of the priest, which is expressed in words, seals the remission of sins, which it accomplishes in the soul." " There is no sin, however grievous, no crime, however enormous, or however frequently repeated, which penance does not remit. Without the intervention of penance we cannot obtain, or even hope for, pardon." " The penitent must also submit himself to the judgment of the priest, who is the vice-gerent of God, to enable him to award a punishment proportioned to his guilt.' — Pp. 239, 240, 242, 245.

The Church of Rome teaches that the absolution of a wicked priest is as valid as that of a pious one. The Council of Trent declares in one of its canons that " if any one says that priests under mortal sin have no power to bind or loose, let him be accursed."

The penitent, therefore, holding such exalted notions of the power of the priest, coming into his presence and in the secrecy of the confessional, unbosoming to him the inmost secrets of the heart and life, secrets that the wife might not reveal to her husband, and thoughts, temptations, possibly partial yieldings, of so delicate a nature that the young maiden would not disclose to her own mother, yet all this must be whispered into the open ear of the confessor, and he in turn " absolves " (?) from

THE FORGIVENESS OF SIN.

sin, and counsels the penitent. What a mighty power such a system places in the hands of a man !

Further, this same penitent that has been forgiven by the priest, enters the church, and he beholds the priest occupying the place of Jesus Christ himself, changing by virtue of his priestly office the bread and the wine into the body and blood of Christ, believing this puts him under the power of the priest.

In proof of the alleged power of the priesthood I quote a passage from the writings of St. Alphonsus Liguori, who is accepted in the Church of Rome as the great Master of Moral Theology. In his work entitled, " Dignity and Duty of a Priest," translated and published but recently in America, London and Dublin, and printed by " the printers of the Apostolic See," Liguori says :—
" The priest has the power of the keys, or the power of delivering sinners from hell, of making them worthy of Paradise, and of changing them from slaves of Satan into the child of God. And God Himself *is obliged to abide by the judgment of His priests*, and either not to pardon, or to pardon, according as they (the priests) refuse to give absolution, provided the penitent is capable of it.

" Were the Redeemer to descend into a church, and sit in a confessional to administer the Sacrament of Penance, and a priest to sit in another confessional, Jesus would say over each penitent, ' I absolve thee,' and the penitent of each would be equally absolved." The same author also says : " Jesus Christ has also given power to His priests to rescue from hell, not only the bodies but also the souls of the faithful."

That the entire doctrinal system and ecclesiastical polity of the Roman Church is planned for the enrichment of its treasury needs but little proof. Note the triple link binding together the mass, indulgences, and purgatory, and see how perfect is the plot for extorting money from the credulous devotee. The Romish doctrine respecting sin has no support in the Bible. The distinction the Church makes between mortal and venial sins is entirely visionary, but it serves well the purpose of the church as it provides for purgatory. And it is the accepted opinion of the doctors of the Church that none who now die go direct to heaven, but are detained in purgatory for an indefinite length of time. Their sufferings, however, in that state are assuaged by what is termed the suffrages of the faithful on earth, that is, prayers, masses, and alms or gifts to the church. Masses, however, for the dead are costly. Vast sums of money are expended for masses for the dead by relatives and friends of the departed, all of which goes to enrich the treasury of the church.

XXV.

ROME AND THE BIBLE

THE attitude of the Church of Rome toward the Bible has always been that of hostility. The first book ever printed in Italy by the Pope's press at Subiaco, near Rome, was in 1465, and from it poured forth a perfect stream of literature of all kinds ; but never a book never a chapter, never a verse of Scripture. Put into the hands of the people, the Church practically says, any book you please, no matter how degrading, but do not on any account let them have the Bible. There are few demoralizing books on the *Index Expurgatorius*, but there are many editions of the Bible.

The attitude and action of the Roman Catholic Church from the fifth century to the twentieth in regard to the Bible may be termed, *determined deadly opposition.* As early as 860, Pope Nicholas I. pronounced against both the Bible and all those who read it ; Gregory VII., in 1703, confirmed the ban ; and Innocent III., in 1198, declared that all who read the Bible should be stoned to death. In 1229 the Council of Toulouse passed a decree against the possession or reading of the Bible. In 1564, Pius IV., when confirming the decrees of the Council of Trent, issued a bull to the same effect with disastrous effect. It was designed to stop the Reformation in Italy, and, coupled with the extermination of all, high and low, known to have embraced it, it had that effect. As a distinguished priest and Professor in

Florence said a few years ago in a lecture on the Bible : " For two hundred years the Bible in Italy was an unknown book." And he added, "Then commenced the decadence—moral, religious, and political—of Italy." In 1600, Clement VIII., who burned Giordano Bruno, decreed that any one found reading the Bible in the vernacular would be sent to the galleys for life.

In England, in the fourteenth century, any one found possessing the Bible of Wycliffe, that " organ of the devil" as he was called, incurred the penalty of death. On the accession of " Bloody Mary " to the throne of England, in 1553, tons of Bibles were used as faggots to light the piles for martyrs.

When the Bible societies were formed, and ever since, the Popes have vied with each other in the ferocity of the bulls they have fulminated against them, Pius VII., in 1816, denounced them as " pestilences to be arrested by any means possible," and Leo XII., in 1825, as " traps and pitfalls." Pius VIII., in 1830, denounced all the Bibles that issued from their printing presses as " centres of pestiferous infection," and Gregory XVI., in 1844, condemned the societies, and instructed the priests to tear up all the Bibles that they could lay their hands on.

Dr. Alexander Robertson tells us that on the accession of " Bloody Mary " to the throne of England, in 1553, there existed a painting in London of King Henry VIII., in which he was represented standing holding in one hand a sceptre, and in the other a Bible, with the words on its cover, *Verbum Dei*. This exhibition of the " Word of God " was so offensive to Papal eyes that it was obliterated, and a pair of gloves painted in its place. Pius IX. was most bitter in his opposition to the reading of the Bible and Bible societies. It was under his reign that Count Guicciardini, Guerra, Guarducci, and many others were banished from Tuscany for reading the Bible. And it was under him that Francesco Madiai and his wife were arrested in Florence, in August, 1851, for reading the Bible, imprisoned in the Bargello for ten months, and then sent to the galleys. And, also, about the same time an English gentleman, Arthur Walker, was arrested for having a Bible in his pocket, and was imprisoned. It was when Pius IX. held sway in the Vatican that the Hon. Dexter A. Hawkins, a prominent lawyer in New York, was sent to Italy to gather some data in regard to education, and while in Rome, the American Consul, ascertaining that Mr. Hawkins had a Bible in his possession, warned him not to let it be known, for, said he, if it is known, I cannot even as American Consul save you from twelve months' imprisonment.

But it may be said that this hostility is directed against Protestant versions, and not against Roman Catholic ones. But such is not the case. The opposition is against the Bible, pure and simple. Catholic Bibles have shared the same fate as Protestant ones when they found their way into popular use. On May 18th, 1849, some three thousand copies of the Catholic New Testament were seized and destroyed in Tuscany. Roman priests are ignorant of the Bible. The Bible is not used as a text-book in the Papal seminaries. Count Campello was trained for the priesthood in the Academy of Noble Ecclesiastics, the highest training College in

Rome, and yet during all his years of study he never even saw a Bible. Catholic Missionaries do not use the Bible, and there is no instance in history of their having put a copy of Holy Scripture into the hands of their converts.

A young man, a very zealous Catholic in a town in Italy, got hold of a New Testament, and took it to the priest. The priest said : " You have got hold of a very bad book. That book was printed in hell." The words awoke the young man's curiosity, and, in spite of the protest of the priest who desired to have it, he took it home to read it. The result was his conversion, and he afterward became an evangelist.

The question often arises in the minds of Protestants, Why are Catholic priests so hostile to the Bible ? Why do they not want their people to read it ? The simple answer is, If they read the Bible, it will set them thinking ; it will awaken thought. And that is opposed to the genius of the Papacy. The Pope demands the *sacrifice of the intellect.* God in the Bible appeals to our reason. He says, " Come, let us reason together." " Prove all things : hold fast that which is good." " Think on these things." I know a Roman Catholic priest—he is a personal friend ; he is being persecuted for his loyalty to the truth, and yet he is in the Church. I have heard of another priest who is anxious that his people should possess the Bible and read it, and he also wants his brother-priests to know it, and preach it, and to comfort the sick with its Divine words. " But," he says, " alas ! I fear that these my wishes will never be realized. And why ? Because the day in which the priests and Catholic believers give themselves to the reading and the study of the Bible, that day will be the last for the Roman Church, for the priests, an for the Papacy." That thought of the Italian priest is in keeping with the words used by Zanardelli, the present Premier of Italy, in a speech made at Brescia : " Woe to the Roman Catholic Church when my countrymen get hold of the Old and New Testaments, then they will know the difference between Jesus Christ and His so-called Vicar."

When the Ecumenical Council, held in the Vatican in 1869-70, was in session, at which the infallibility of the Pope was decreed, the following curious incident occurred. Dollinger and Dupanloup, in supporting their arguments against the proposed new dogma, wished to refer to some passages of Scripture ; but no one had a Bible in the whole Council, nor could one be procured for them within the bounds of the Church, so one had to be borrowed from the Protestant chaplain of the Prussian Embassy !

As a noted writer has said : " The ignorance of the Roman Catholic clergy of the Bible is only equalled by their hostility to it." The two go hand in hand. Padre Curci, the learned Jesuit, who died a few years ago in a convent at Fiesole, to which he had been banished by the Vatican for his liberal writings, said in his work *Vaticano Regio* : " If theological study in general has waned and degenerated amongst our clergy, biblical study has been entirely abandoned. The activity of the Protestants in the study of the Bible, which ought to be to us a noble incentive, has been made a pretext for calumny to such an extent that already in some large dioceses an understanding is allowed to circulate quietly amongst the younger clergy that, as the study of the Bible is a Protestant affair, it would be a curse to any one to engage in it."

AFRAID OF THE LIGHT.

Why is it that the Romish Church cuts out the second Commandment entirely from their Catechisms ; and then to make the number good makes two Commandments of the tenth ?

The Commandment which they do not wish their children to learn is as follows :—

"*Thou shalt not make unto thee any graven image, or any likeness of anything that is in heaven above, or that is in the earth beneath, or that is in the water under the earth ; thou shalt not bow down thyself to them, nor serve them : for I the Lord thy God am a jealous God, visiting the iniquity, of the fathers upon the children unto the third and fourth generation of them that hate Me, and showing mercy unto thousands of them that love Me, and keep My commandments.* —Exodus xx. 4-6. It is the same both in the Douay and Authorized Versions.

What right has any Church to mutilate Holy Scripture? Against such the malediction of Jesus Christ is pronounced : " If any man shall take away from the words of the book, God shall take away his part out of the book of life. —Rev. xxii. 19.

XXVI.

ROME AND INDULGENCES

THE doctrine of Indulgences is a delicate one with Roman Catholics, having been the occasion of so much scandal to the Church, and yet at the same time such an exhaustless source of revenue, that they pass over it as lightly as they can, softening and minimizing its peculiarities. An indulgence is a remission of the temporal punishment due to venial sin, and also to mortal sin, after the eternal punishment has been remitted. According to the teaching of Rome, when the " penitent " receives absolution, he is delivered from the eternal punishment due, *i.e.*, hell, but not free from the temporal punishment due. This must be borne by himself either in this world or in purgatory; and Indulgences are the means by which it may be in part or in whole remitted.

These Indulgences are dispensed by the authority of the Pope. He holds the keys to this " heavenly treasure," assuming the prerogative of God Himself. For who can forgive sins but God only. Some Romish writers deny that Indulgences confer the pardon of sin. They are very sensitive at that point, especially in view of Protestant criticism. But historic facts are abundant in proof that the above statement is true. The Popes of Rome have expressly affirmed that the recipients of an Indulgence " obtain the fullest pardon of all their sins." And the late Pope Leo XIII., in his

Encyclical of September 1st, 1883, granted to all the faithful " the full remission of all their sins."

The sacrament of Penance and the doctrine of Indulgences, taken together, present a complete view of Rome's system of pardon. Under the one, the *eternal* punishment of sin in hell is remitted, and under the other the *temporary* punishment of sin in purgatory is remitted.

The doctrine of Indulgences is one of the many novelties of the Roman Church. In the early church it was unknown. The pretentious claim that the doctrines of the Church are the same as in the days of Christ and the Apostles, or even in the early age of the church, is without foundation. It was not until the fourteenth century that the idea of mitigating temporal pains inflicted by the Church was extended to the abbreviating of the time to be spent in purgatory. In this way Indulgences began to be considered as helpful to the dead as to the living.

In the sixteenth century the sale of Indulgences had become a recognized traffic in the Church. Leo X. wished money partly to finish the building of St. Peter's, and partly to meet his extravagances ; accordingly, he published Indulgences which professed to secure the full remission of sins, and these found a ready sale in the ecclesiastical market of Europe. They were farmed out by the Pope to the highest bidder, and the price was paid beforehand to the Pontiff.

In Germany the purchaser was Albert, Archbishop of Mainz and Magdeburg, a prelate notorious for his extravagance ; and his agent was the famous or rather infamous Tetzel. In this way a most indecent and scandalous traffic was carried on by the agents of the Pope, and every kind of sin had its price in money.

Early in the sixteenth century the Church of Rome actually published to the world a book entitled " *Taxae Penitentiariae*," in which were quoted the prices to be paid for the pardon of all conceivable kinds of sin and crime, even the worst. The genuineness of this book has been denied. But the fact has been abundantly established, and the repeated editions prepared under Papal sanction leave no doubt in regard to it. "*Janus*." It may be said that the Church has changed in regard to such things. In reply, we say that the late Pius IX. was in the habit of sending to Sicily, up to the year 1868, a Bull which contained " an explicit catalogue of crimes with the sums required to receive forgiveness." By means of this Bull the Pope authorized all Father Confessors in Sicily to condone crimes for a pecuniary consideration. A burglar or bandit would appear before the priest telling him he had pilfered or spent 1,000 lire. " No matter," the priest would say under the Bull. " if you have preserved a portion of the spoils for the Church ; " thus a compromise was easily arrived at. The burglar paid the Pope a tax, and the Pope in return absolved the burglar. In the Bull mentioned there was a complete list of all imaginable crimes—rape, robbery, murder ; nothing was omitted, and side by side with each crime was the price set upon it.

The basis upon which the indulgence and mass traffic is worked is the alleged *Treasury of Merits* scheme.

(Speech of Signor Tajani, Minister of Justice in the Italian Government, on the 11th July, 1875. Reported in *Times*. ')

148 FROM ROME TO CHRIST.

That is the shrewdest piece of religious financiering ever produced in the Vatican.

The Pope argues thus: One drop of Christ's blood was sufficient for the redemption of the whole world, therefore all the rest that he shed, together with the merits and prayers of all the saints, over and above what were needed for their own salvation, constitutes an *inexhaustible treasury or bank*, on which the Pope has a right to draw, and these drafts are applied in payment for the relief or release of souls in purgatory. But these drafts cost money. Millions go into the coffers of the Church every year as the result of this scheme. It is so arranged also that anyone who obtains an Indulgence can apply its merits to himself, or transfer it to some other, living or dead. The plan is based on the alleged claim that the Pope controls the treasury. He holds the key. He is the Dispenser of grace. He opens and no man can shut ; and he shuts and no man can open. But every turn of the key implies a deposit of hard cash.

XXVII.

THE CENTRAL DOCTRINE OF THE CHURCH OF ROME OVERTHROWN AT THE BAR OF REASON AND HOLY SCRIPURE

THE CLAIM THAT THE PRIEST, IN THE MASS, ACTUALLY CHANGES THE WAFER INTO THE LIVING CHRIST, BODY AND BLOOD, BONES AND SINEWS, BREATHING LUNGS AND BEATING HEART, SOUL AND DIVINITY, THE REAL SON OF MAN, AND SON OF GOD, IS ABSOLUTELY OVERTHROWN BY THE FOLLOWING PLAIN FACTS :—

The inspired Apostle in the Epistle to the Hebrews declares that " Jesus Christ is the same yesterday, and to-day, and forever ' (Heb. 13 : 8). He died ONCE for our sins, therefore He never can die again. He says Himself : " I am He that liveth, and was dead ; and, behold, I am alive for evermore ' (Rev. 1 : 18). Now, over against these inspired statements, is the Romish *claim* that wherever or whenever a priest says mass every wafer in his hand, upon the consecration thereof, becomes a veritable, actual living Christ, the same Christ who died on the Cross, and who now is at the right hand of God. It is to be understood also, as the Church teaches, that the wafer is not a *figurative representation* of Christ but Jesus Christ in His entirety. In proof that I am not misrepresenting this monstrous claim of the Roman Church, I will quote Canon I. of the Council of Trent in 1551 : " Whosoever shall deny that in the most holy sacrament of the Eucharist there are truly, really, and substantially contained the body and blood of our Lord Jesus Christ, together with His soul and divinity, and consequently Christ entire ; but shall affirm that He is present therein only in a sign or figure, or by His power ; let him be accursed."

Further, the Christ thus made by the priest is eaten by him, given to the communicant at the altar and eaten by him, and thus during the centuries millions and billions of Christs have been made. Now the question arises, WHERE ARE ALL THESE MAN-MADE CHRISTS ? Where are the myriad Christs that have been made on all the Roman altars throughout the world ? If the doctrine of transubstantiation is true they are all alive.

Here is another vital point in this connection that has never been satisfactorily met : the wafer that has been changed into the body of Christ is subject to decomposition. It *does* decompose. It enters the stomach and passes through the ordinary process of digestion and decomposition the same as any other material digestible substance, and thus it becomes *corrupt*. Whereas it is positively and clearly declared in the Bible, and it is the same in the Douay or Catholic as in the Authorized or Revised version, that *the body of Christ should not see corruption* (Ps. 16 : 10 ; Acts 2 : 27, 13 : 37). Thus we see that the Church of Rome in her claim that the wafer is the living Christ, is arrayed against reason, common sense, and the expressed deliverances of the Word of God in her own Scriptures.

Here is another fact that staggers faith in this bold and unwarranted assumption : the consecrated wafers that are not used in the communion service at the church are placed in the small receptacle on the altar

ROMISH DOCTRINE OVERTHROWN. 151

called the "tabernacle," and when they are kept there for a given time, and begin to decompose, are taken by the priest and consumed, and the ashes consigned to a sacred place. *Think of Jesus Christ in His humanity and divinity being burned* !

The following incident occurred in the city of Rochester, N.Y., about three years ago from the time of this writing. In the State Industrial School there was a young Catholic girl whose curiosity became aroused in regard to the wafer, and the wonderful change that she was taught takes place on its consecration. She could not understand how it could be the real body and blood of Christ. She began to *think*, to *question* in her mind how it could be. That was where she broke with the teachings of the Church. For a Catholic is not allowed to raise an inquiry in regard to any tenet of the Church. Absolute surrender of the intellect to the will of the Pope is the inflexible rule. This poor girl, however, ventured to *think* and *reason* on the subject, which led her to the rash act of taking the wafer from her tongue while kneeling at the altar and receiving the sacrament. She took it to her room to examine it, but in doing so her conscience smote her as having done a sacrilegious thing. She told one of the lady superintendents, a Catholic lady, what she had done, who informed the priest. The poor girl was brought before him and charged with having committed a great sin. The entire Institution was thrown into a great commotion over the incident. What remained of the wafer was burned by the priest, and the ashes entombed in holy ground.

The above incident was told the writer by the chief superintendent of the Institution.

XXVIII.

HALF COMMUNION

DO Roman Catholics ever receive the sacrament of the Lord's Supper? We answer: No, they do not. For several hundred years no Roman Catholic has ever received from the hands of the priest the holy Eucharist as Christ instituted it, and ordained that it should be received. The bread only, in the form of a wafer, is given to the laity, and the priests themselves unless they are officiating in the Mass. whereas, Jesus in giving the cup to His disciples as they sat at the table on that memorable night laid special stress upon their receiving the wine. I quote four passages from the New Testament. In Matthew's Gospel, 26 : 27-28, we read : " And he took the cup, and gave thanks, saying, DRINK YE ALL OF IT ; for this is my blood of the new covenant which is shed for many for the remission of sins." In Mark's Gospel, 14 : 23-24, we read : " And he took the cup, and when he had given thanks, he gave it to them : AND THEY ALL DRANK OF IT. And he said unto them, This is my blood of the new covenant, which is shed for many." In Luke's Gospel, 22 : 17-20, we read : " And he took the cup, and gave thanks, and said : Take this, and divide it among yourselves; saying, This cup is the new covenant in my blood, which is shed for you.'" We turn now to Paul's first letter to the Corinthian church, 1 Cor., 11 : 25-27, and we read : " After the same manner also he took the cup, when he had supped, saying : This cup is the new covenant in my blood ; this do ye, as oft as ye drink it, in remembrance of me. For as often as ye DRINK THIS CUP, ye do show the Lord s death till he come. Whosoever shall . . . DRINK THIS CUP of the Lord unworthily shall be guilty of the . . . . blood of the Lord."

We see, then, from those passages, that if either of the elements are to be dispensed with, it should be the bread rather than the wine. For the wine is a symbol of the blood. And the blood is the life. Special emphasis is placed upon the blood of Christ all through the New Testament. " We have redemption through his blood," says Paul, " the forgiveness of sins, according to the riches of his grace." " But now in Christ Jesus ye who sometimes were far off are made nigh by the blood of Christ." " Unto him that loved us, and washed us from our sins in his own blood.' " By his own blood he entered in once into the holy place, having obtained eternal redemption for us." " The blood of Jesus Christ his Son cleanseth us from all sin." " Without the shedding of blood there is no remission." Thus we see that the covenant of blood, the sacrificial, atoning blood is the focus of revelation, in which the Old Testament and the New are one.

Has the Roman Church always refused the wine to the laity, administering only a half communion ? By no means. One of their own writers affirms " that in the Latin Church, for above a thousand years, the body of Christ and the blood of Christ were separately given, the body apart and the blood apart, after the consecration of the mysteries." So Aquinas, one of the greatest fathers of the Church, affirms : " According to the ancient custom of the Church, all men, as they communicated in the body, so they communicated in the blood ; which also to this day is kept in some churches." Indeed, there was a law for communion in both kinds ; for Pope Gelasius says : "We find that some, having received a portion only of the holy body, do abstain from the cup of the holy blood ; who doubtless should receive the entire sacrament wholly ; because the division of one and the same mystery cannot be without very great sacrilege." Many other similar testimonies might be given. Even in the year 1414 the Council of Constance declared that Christ instituted the sacrament in both kinds ; that in the primitive church both kinds were received by the laity as well as the clergy ; but for the purpose of avoiding certain *dangers and scandals* half communion was resorted to, and now communion in both kinds is called an *error*, and all priests are to be punished if administering it as Christ commanded they should. The Council of Trent makes the same concession as to its having been ordained by Christ and commanded to be received in both kinds, and yet anathematizes any one that believes half communion is wrong. Jesus once told the Jews that they made void the commandment of God by their tradition. If he were on the earth today he would say the same of the papacy.

THE ADORATION OF THE WAFER.

The priest during the celebration of the Mass, having repeated over the wafer the words, "*This is my body*," falls down on his knees and adores it. He worships that very thing which a short time before was taken out of the oven, a bit of unleavened paste in the form of a wafer. He gives to it the supreme worship both of

HALF COMMUNION.

body and mind, as he might to Christ Himself. The following is the English of the very words in their Missal, the book the priest reads from during the Mass : " Having uttered the words of consecration, the priest, immediately falling on his knees, adores the consecrated host : he rises, shows it to the people, places it on the corporale, and again adores it. When the wine is consecrated, the priest in like manner, falling on his knees, adores it, rises, shows it to the people, puts the cup in its place, covers it over, and again adores it. The priest, rising up after he has adored it himself, lifts it up as high as he conveniently can, and, with eyes fixed upon it, shows it, to be devoutly adored by the people."

If Christ were visibly present, they could not bestow more acts of worship on Him than they do to the wafer.

XXIX.

A STRIKING PARALLEL

IN the forty-fourth chapter of Isaiah we have the following description of an idol: "The smith with the tongs both worketh in the coals, and fashioneth it with hammers, and worketh it with the strength of his arms. The carpenter stretcheth out his rule; he marketh it out with a line, he fitteth it with planes, and he marketh it out with the compass, and maketh it after the figure of a man, according to the beauty of a man; that it may remain in the house. He heweth him down cedars, and taketh the cypress and the oak: he planteth an ash, and the rain doth nourish it. Then shall it be for a man to burn: for he will take thereof, and warm himself; yea, he kindleth it, and baketh bread; yea, he maketh a god, and worshippeth it; he maketh it a graven image, and falleth down thereto. He burneth part thereof in the fire; with part thereof he eateth flesh; he roasteth roast, and is satisfied: yea, he warmeth himself, and saith, Aha, I am warm, I have seen the fire: and the residue thereof he maketh a god, even his graven image: he falleth down unto it, and worshippeth it, and prayeth unto it, and saith, Deliver me; for thou art my god." The parallel between this and making Christ out of the wafer, and worshipping it, is very striking.

The farmer soweth wheat, it grows, it ripens, is reaped, and is threshed; it is ground at the mill, it is sifted with

A STRIKING PARALLEL.

a sieve; with a part thereof the fowls and cattle are fed; another part is taken and baked by the maid in the kitchen, yet it is no God; it is given to the priest who handles it and crosses it, and yet it is no god; he pronounces over a few words in Latin, when, lo, instantly it becomes the supreme God! He then falls down before it and prays to it, saying, "Thou art my God." He lifts it up to the people, and cries in Latin—" Behold the Lamb of God, that taketh away the sin of the world." The whole congregation fall down and worship it, and cry, " My fault, my fault, my very great fault."

If that described by the prophet Isaiah is idolatry, by what name will you call that which transpires whenever the Mass is offered up?

XXX.

PRIESTLY RULE UNFAVORABLE TO NATIONAL PROSPERITY

WHY is that during the last three centuries, throughout the civilized world, the intellectual, commercial, and national greatness of those peoples has been secured and developed through the prevalence and predominance of Protestant Christianity ? Why is it that Catholic writers (Dublin Review, October, 1877) admit the greater prosperity of Protestant communities, remarking : " Catholicity never yet claimed to be a wealth producing agency." The fact is the Church of Rome cannot raise nations in the scale of civilization. The evident reason is that evangelical Protestantism emphasises the direct relationship of men to God. Whereas the Roman Catholic system emphasises their relationship to the priest.

" The Catholic Religion," says Mr Lecky, the historian, " is exceedingly unfavourable to independence of character and to independence of intellect, which are the first conditions of national progress. It softens, but it also weakens the character, and it produces habits of thought and life not favorable to industrial activity, and extremely opposed to political freedom."

Mr Lecky continues : " No class of men by their principles, and their modes of life and of thought, are less fitted for political leadership than Catholic priests. It is scarcely possible that they should be sincerely attached to tolerance, intellectual activity, or political freedom."

PRIESTLY RULE UNFAVORABLE. 159

And he adds, " It may indeed be safely asserted that, under the conditions of modern life, no country will ever play a great and honorable part in the world if the policy of its rulers, or the higher education of its people, is subject to the control of the Catholic priesthood."

" That is certainly the condition of Catholic Ireland. All the Catholic schools are in the hands of the priests. Not only are the laity excluded from all voice in educational matters ; but also, the hospitals being entirely in the priests' hands, there is scarcely any scope for private initiative in works of charity amongst Catholics in Ireland ; and social life is thus robbed of one of its most beneficent charms."

A few years ago, a bright and eloquent young Irish lawyer, who had been brought up a Roman Catholic, Michael J. F. M'Carthy, Esq., delivered a lecture in Edinburgh on " Catholic Ireland and Protestant Scotland—A Contrast." It is an eminently suggestive production. He says : " In 1801 the population of Scotland was only 1,608,420 ; in 1841 it was 2,620,184 ; and in 1901 its population was 4,472,103. The rise was not a spasmodic one, but a steady increase over the entire century, every decennial period showing a uniform excess over the preceding period.

" Apply the same test to Catholic Ireland, and what do we find ? In 1841 the population of Ireland was 8,175,124, or nearly treble the population of Scotland in that year, but in 1901 it had fallen to 4,458,775 ; and Ireland to-day contains over 200,000 less people than Scotland !

" People enquire, How much of Ireland's misery is racial ? I answer, None of it ! Notice that portion of

160 FROM ROME TO CHRIST.

the United Kingdom which has been called 'the Celtic fringe.' Northern Ireland, Southern Ireland, Scotland, Wales, Manxland, and Cornwall are the Celtic districts of the United Kingdom.

"Northern Ireland, Scotland, Wales, Manxland and Cornwall are Celtic and Protestant, and they are prosperous. Southern Ireland is Celtic and Catholic, and it is not prosperous.

"Is it not clear, therefore, that it is to religion and not to race that Southern Ireland must trace her unhappy condition? Do we not also see that the same religion produces the same consequences amongst races who are not akin to the Irish."

XXXI.

A DAMAGING DOGMA

THE doctrine of Papal Infallibility is seriously embarrassed by the fact that it isr etroactive.

That is, the dogma constitutes not only the present Pope and all his successors infallible, but it includes all his predecessors, not excepting such monsters of iniquity as Pope Alexander VI. the Nero of the Papacy, one of the vilest criminals on record. In proof of the damaging facts that confront this dogma we give a quotation from one of the highest historical authorities in the Roman Church, Cardinal Baronius, the Ultramontane annalist in the tenth century. He writes :—
" What was then the semblance of the Holy Roman Church ? As foul as it could be : when harlots, superior in power, as in profligacy, governed at Rome, at whose will Sees were transferred, bishops were appointed, and, what is horrible and awful to say, their paramours were intruded into the See of Peter ; false Pontiffs who are set down in the catalogue of Roman Pontiffs merely for chronological purposes ; for who can venture to say that persons thus basely intruded by such courtezans were legitimate Roman Pontiffs ? No mention can be found of election or subsequent consent on the part of the clergy, all the Canons were buried in oblivion, the decrees of the Popes stifled, the ancient traditions put under ban, and the old customs, sacred rites, and former usages in the election of the Chief Pontiff were quite abolished. Mad lust, relying on wordly power, thus

claimed all its own, goaded only by the sting of ambition. Christ was then in a deep sleep in the ship, when the ship itself was covered by the waves and these great tempests were blowing. And what seemed worse, there were no disciples to wake Him with their cries, as He slept, for all were snoring. You can imagine as you please what sort of presbyters and deacons were chosen as cardinals by these monsters."

This period covered a space of sixty years, and the reigns of thirteen Popes. But Gilbert Genebrard, Archbishop of Air (1537-1597), writing of the same era says :—" This age has been unfortunate, in so far that during nearly a hundred and fifty years about *fifty Popes* have fallen away from the virtues of their predecessors, being apostates, or apostatical, rather than apostolical." That is to say, about *one-fifth* of all the Popes who have ever sat at Rome are hereby charged with grievous criminality.

In view of these astounding, well established facts, which might be increased or multiplied a thousand fold, what becomes of the boasted holiness and personal infallibility of the Papacy ?

The most serious obstacle that the honest-minded Roman Catholic inquirer has to encounter is the flaws or breaks in the Papal succession. There are gaps there that never can be bridged. In the long catalogue of Popes there are thirty-one that historians mark " doubtful," and twenty-seven classed " invalid."

Further, the doctrine of " *intention* " which is vital and fundamental in their teaching unsettles everything from the baptism of an infant to the ordination of a

A DAMAGING DOGMA.

bishop or the changing the wafer into the Lord Jesus Christ. The virtue of the act all hinges upon the "*intention*" of the officiating priest.

In the Roman Catholic Church the *intention of the priest* is held to be essential to the valid celebration of the Sacraments. This the Council of Trent decreed in its eleventh canon: "If any one shall say that in ministers, while they effect and confer the Sacraments, there is not required the *intention* at least of doing what the Church does, let him be accursed." The same principle has been advocated and set forth by several popes. The same doctrine is taught in the Public Mass Book or Missal, from which the priest reads on the altar. So abused has this principle generally become in the Roman Church, that by its consequences it must be declared to be greatly detrimental to the cause of the Christian religion. "If a wicked priest, for instance, should baptize a child without an *inward intention* to baptize him it would follow that the baptism was null and void for want of the *intention*."

It follows, therefore, from the teaching of this doctrine, that no one in the Roman faith can be positively certain that any of the Sacraments are duly administered.

If this doctrine or teaching of *intention* were followed to its legitimate or logical conclusion, it would unsettle the very foundation of the Papacy.

XXXII.

PETER AND THE ROCK

Thou art the Christ, the Son of the living God . . . Upon this Rock I will build My Church. Matt. 16: 16, 18.

*ON these sentences, or the truth they contain, has been built up the mighty Church of Christ, and, strange to say, on the same simple words has that church been divided. From one of these clauses the Church of Rome pretends to derive authority for the imperial power of the Pope—not only over temporal affairs, but over the spiritual and eternal interests of the whole world. To sustain its claim to be the one and only true Church on earth, Rome has fought and struggled for many a century.

"Thou art Peter, and upon this rock I will build My church;" and "I will give unto you the Keys of the Kingdom. Whatsoever thou shalt bind on earth shall be bound in heaven, and whatsoever thou shalt loose on earth shalt be loosed in heaven." Volumes have been written on these few words. Multitudes of lives have been lost and millions of money have been spent in maintaining the Roman view. Let us approach this subject cautiously, reverently, and with unbiased minds.

Our Lord's ministry was approaching its tragic close. For more than two years he had taught the people and wrought miracles. In all parts of Palestine men had had abundant opportunity to hear and see Him. Everybody had discussed Him. The dreaded and awful moment had arrived when the meaning of His mission must be made known to the disciples. They must be prepared for His crucifixion,

---

*A Sermon delivered in New York Presbyterian Church, New York City, by the Pastor, Rev. Duncan J. McMillan, D. D.

PETER AND THE ROCK. 165

about to be accomplished, and for the great responsibilities that would suddenly fall on their shoulders. Jesus approaches the subject cautiously. To what purpose had He wrought out His marvelous earthly ministry? What is the state of the popular mind after all? "Who do men say that I, the Son of Man, am?" What is their estimate? From the disciples comes the ready reply: "Some say, John the Baptist; some say, Elijah; some, Jeremiah." Still further opinions diverged, but all agreed that Jesus was a reincarnation of one of the great prophets, and all assigned Him the highest rank among men.

Even these human estimates of His character and purposes were of interest to Him. The most valuable estimate, however, was not that of the multitude, but that of the few friends who stood close to Him, were competent to judge, and had views of their own. In the storm-tossed ship when He came to them and quieted the turbulent sea, they worshipped Him, saying: "Of a truth Thou art the Son of God." But would they dare assert that conviction now, that they were safe on land, in the face of the popular sentiment? "Who say *ye* that I am?" It was an appeal from the judgment of the multitudes to that of experts; not only that, it was a question leading up to a new and glorious era, whose portals were to swing wide open there and then.

Were the disciples upon whom the whole new movement must rest prepared in mind and heart for this fuller revelation of truth? Would they be brave and true enough? "Who say *ye* that I am?"

In every company of men there is always a spokesman. The chairman or some member of the committee reports for the committee. So among the disciples sometimes one, sometimes another, spoke for the rest. On one occasion (Mark 9: 38) John was the spokesman and said: "Master, we saw one casting out devils in Thy name," etc. At another time (John 14: 5) Thomas was their spokesman and said: "Lord, we know not whither Thou goest," etc. Again, Philip was spokesman (John 14: 8) and said: "Lord, show us the Father, and it sufficeth us." And on another occasion (John 14: 22) Judas spoke for the others and said: "Lord, how is it that Thou wilt show thyself unto us, and not unto the world?" So among the disciples there was no difference in rank. On the present occasion, Peter spoke for the rest, saying just what they had all said a few days before in the ship: "Thou art the Christ, the Son of the living God." Here is the gist of the Apostles' Creed, the crystalization of all the Christian doctrines, the basis of all theology, the foundation principle on which all church life rests. Then follow those wonderful words of our Lord—like a belated beatitude— crowning that glorious confession of faith with a divine benediction, and then, as if to keep Peter from being puffed up with pride, Christ said: "Flesh and blood hath not revealed this unto thee"—that is, You did not evolve this out of your own mind and heart—"but My Father which is in heaven" has revealed it unto you. "And I say unto thee that thou art Peter, and upon this rock I will build My Church."

While it is true that this is the first use of the word "Church" it is by no means the first use of the word "Rock" as the foundation on which the superstructure of God's kingdom on earth should rest. And, during the earliest centuries of the Christian era, no other

PETER AND THE ROCK.

significance attached to these words than that Christ and faith in Him as the Son of God, was the basal principle—the foundation stone of the Church on earth. And, in all probability, no other meaning would ever have been advanced but for the remarkable claims of the Church of Rome, which were first set forth *three centuries after Christ*. At that time the Bishop of the Church of Rome gave a new meaning to the words which Jesus addressed to Peter, wresting them from their obvious significance. He claimed that these words constituted a new, divine commission to Peter by which *he* was made the rock on which the Church was to be built—notwithstanding Paul's emphatic declaration in Eph. 2: 20, "Ye are built upon the foundation of the Apostles and prophets, Jesus Christ Himself being the chief cornerstone." He maintained that Peter was to be Primate of the Kingdom of God on earth, in the face of our Lord's emphatic statement to the mother of James and John that "To sit on my right hand and on my left is not mine to give," etc.; that Peter was to be head over the Church though it had been expressly written of *Jesus* Himself "*He hath been made Head over all things to the Church;*" and that Peter was to have power to forgive sins and to pronounce condemnation on whom he chose, and yet it had been expressly stated: "*no man forgiveth sins save God alone.*"

Further, it was claimed that Peter became the first pastor or bishop of the Church of Rome, and that all these divine functions and prerogatives which were declared to have been conferred upon him passed on to his successors at Rome who, since the *fifth century*, have been called Pope. Upon this pretension the whole fabric of the Roman Catholic Church rests, and the 230,000,000 members are held together by it. The Roman Catholics are compelled to accept the teachings of the Pope, upon pain of loss of their souls, while 247,000,000 Protestants deny these claims and declare that there is no scriptural authority for them.

Jesus said: "Thou art Peter, and upon this Rock I will build my Church." Upon what rock? The Pope of Rome says "Peter" means a rock, and that Christ meant that He would build His Church on Peter.

It is rather humiliating to have to juggle about little words in carrying on great controversies. But since that is the way the Pope justifies himself in his office and maintains his claims, we must look into the matter. Yes: "*Petros*" does mean a stone. But Jesus did not say: "Upon this *Petros*." He said "Upon this *Petra*." Not much difference? No, not much; yet the whole controversy, in my judgment, rests upon that difference. Let us illustrate the difference. A ship is wrecked on a *petra*—not on a *petros*. The stonemason lays each *petros* in its place; but no man is called a rock-mason, for God alone lays the *petra*. If a Greek should speak of that great mass which forms the framework of Morningside Heights he would call it *petra*, but if he should refer to an individual fragment which is placed in a wall, or a smaller one that a boy might throw at a bird, he would call it *petros*. A prominent building on Fifth avenue has a fine foundation built of stones, each of which is a *petros;* but those walls rest on a great, broad, underlying rock which is a *petra*. Now if you will examine the New Testament you will find that on three different occasions (including this one) Jesus called Simon "*Petros*."

And that word does not occur elsewhere in the New Testament.

But if you will look for *Petra*, you will find it *twenty times*. In *every instance* it refers either directly or typically to Christ: as for example in the case of the wise man who built his house on a *petra*, "and it fell not," etc. (Matt. 7:24) ; Rom. 9:33, "Behold I lay in Zion a foundation,—a *petra* of offence;" and I. Cor. 10:4, "They did all drink of that spiritual *petra*—and that *petra* was Christ."

If we turn to the Greek lexicons, which are for classical use and have no theological bias whatever, the case is strengthened. Liddell and Scott's says: "There is no example in good authors of *petra* in the significance of *petros*, a single stone." If we go to the Old Testament Scriptures, the Rock which Moses smote, out of which the life-saving water flowed for Israel in the Wilderness, it is *petra*. But time would fail us to multiply the instances.

Let us inquire what Peter himself understood about it. Let us see whether, with all his natural forwardness and self-assertion, he understood that he had been made superior to the others by these words or attached any personal significance to them. It is remarkable that Mark who wrote his gospel under Peter's direction, if not by his dictation, does not mention the matter at all, and does not record any reference to either the rock or the keys. He does, however, record Peter's confession: "Thou art the Christ," etc., though he says nothing about the rest of the conversation. Neither does Luke, neither does John. Matthew alone records the words. They were evidently spoken, or Matthew would not have recorded them. But they have no such significance as the Roman Catholic Church attaches to them, else the other evangelists could not have omitted them.

The Apostle Paul certainly did not so understand the words of our Lord, for he says: "For other foundation can no man lay, than that which is laid, which is Jesus Christ." He also puts all the apostles, including Peter, on a common level, when he refers to "the foundation of the apostles and prophets, Jesus Christ Himself being the chief cornerstone." And Peter himself (I. Pet. 2:8) refers to the stone, rejected by the builders which became the Head of the corner and a rock (*petra*) of offence. No one will deny that this "*petra* of offence" is Christ.

Is it at all conceivable that Jesus, who knew what was in man, would have meant to say that upon Peter as a rock he would build His Church, and that the gates of Hell shall not prevail against it; and then in the very next breath say to the same Peter—"*Get thee behind Me, Satan*"?

What kind of a principal foundation-stone would such a vacillating man make? A man who some months later forsook his Lord and Master and fled from the scene of the crucifixion with the rest of them, after having, only the night before, denied Him?

Then what was our Lord's real meaning by these words? Why evidently and very simply this: "Thou art Petros"—a stone that will go into the foundation— "but upon *this petra*"—using the word as they and everybody else in the Old and New Testament times had used it—referring to Himself, the Son of God. "Upon this *petra* will I build My Church." Just as at another time, he referred to Himself when He said: "Destroy *this* temple, and in three days I will raise it up."

PETER AND THE ROCK.

If we look at the conversation from another point of view, the grammatical, we cannot escape this construction. Christ Himself was the subject and the only subject of the conversation. "Who do men say that I am?" "Thou art the Christ," etc. "Blessed art thou, Simon Barjona, for flesh and blood hath not revealed it," etc. It would have been ungrammatical and confusing to change the subject from our Lord to Peter, and then back from Peter to our Lord again, in that one complex sentence.

Now notice another difficulty of the Romish construction. Christ says: "Upon this *petra* I will build My Church and the gates of Hell shall not prevail against it." But they so prevailed against Peter that very day, that Jesus said to him: "*Get thee behind Me, Satan.*" And Peter fell before temptation several times later on in the Gospel narrative, as we have already seen. No, Jesus did not abdicate in favor of Peter, nor surrender a single one of His prerogatives in favor of him or anyone else.

But perhaps some one will ask: "What about the keys?" Jesus said unto Peter: "And I will give unto thee the keys of the kingdom of heaven." What is meant by the "kingdom of heaven"? Certainly the reign of gospel truth in the world—the Church of God on earth. And what are the keys?" We understand them to be instruments for opening closed doors. The language here is therefore rhetorical. What doors were closed? Jesus had said a little while before to the Gentile Syrophenician woman, that He was "sent only to the lost sheep of the house of Israel," implying that the Gentiles were locked out of the pale of the covenant. He had said to the twelve when He sent them out two years before (Matt. 10: 5, 6) "Go not into the way of the Gentiles, and into any of the cities of the Samaritans enter ye not; but go rather to the lost sheep of the house of Israel. And as ye go, preach, saying, The kingdom of heaven is at hand." This door was not to be opened until Jesus had completed his work as a Jew, fulfilling all the Jewish types and symbols; until the middle wall of partition should be broken down in His great atoning work; until He should, at the very end of it all, cry, "It is finished!" and the veil of the temple should be rent in twain from the top to the bottom, and the door into the Holy of Holies should be laid wide open. It was not until after the Resurrection that Jesus broadened the commission of his disciples so as to extend it beyond the Jewish boundaries and open the gates of life to the Gentiles by saying: "Go ye into all the world and preach the gospel to every creature."

Then, in the division of the work among the apostles by the appointment of Jesus, it fell to Peter to open the door at Pentecost by that powerful sermon by which three thousand of his hearers were converted at once. It was to Peter, also, that the vision came at Joppa of a sheet let down by its four corners wherein were all manner of beasts and creeping things, with the instruction to "rise, slay and eat." Peter said: "Not so, Lord, for I have never eaten anything common or unclean." But the Lord said: "What I have cleansed, call thou not common." Then understood Peter that he was authorized to open the doors of the kingdom to the Gentiles, which he did at the house of Cornelius in Caesarea, and which he and Paul and others did ever after. The doors were never afterward shut, and the keys have never since been in demand.

PETER AND THE ROCK. 173

That the "keys" meant any special pre-eminence for Peter among the apostles or in the councils of the Church above the others does not at all appear. Nor can the Roman view be sustained by any Scriptural or historical warrant. Certainly Paul did not so regard Peter, for he "*withstood him to the face, for he was to be blamed.*" And Paul never "took it back." Nor has history ever justified Peter in that controversy, or condemned Paul's attitude. And when the first council was held at Jerusalem, Peter's predominance would, if ever, have been recognized or asserted. But no; it was James, not Peter, who was called to preside; and as for Peter being pastor or bishop of the Church in Rome, there is not a scrap of scriptural evidence that he ever saw Rome, and if he did, it was not Rome but Jerusalem that was the City of God. Rome was Nero's city.

Peter certainly had much to do with the organization of the infant Church in Palestine, and other local churches. Jesus did not prescribe any special form of government but left that whole matter so that church organization might be adapted to local conditions and the exigencies that might arise.

Peter as well as Paul and the other apostles had much to do with constituting churches, and ordaining their officers, elders, deacons, etc., and formulating church ordinances by which church members might be bound together, and refractory and unworthy ones loosed or disciplined and dismissed. Jesus gave him the assurance of the divine help, blessing and sanction in this necessary part of his work. And so far we can see, God was pleased to bless the arrangements for such things by the apostles in those days, and has ever since blessed all branches of the Church of which

Christ is the living Head of every denomination and under every form and order of government, by which men and women bind themselves by covenant vows, and by which Church authority and discipline have been exercised, whether by Church sessions or bishops, or councils, by whatever name they may be called.

I need not dwell on this part of the Lord's remarkable benediction. He did not say "*whom*soever you bind," etc. He did not refer to persons at all, but using the neuter gender—"*What*soever." He provided for the temporal organization and material affairs of the infant Church. And by the presence and blessing of Jesus Christ, the only Head of the Church, it has been led on to constant victory. It has had to defend itself vigorously against many enemies down through all centuries, but it has never been overcome by them, nor shall the gates of Hell ever prevail against it.

What is Said About the Book by Distinguished Men of Both Continents:

The Rev. Dr. Clifford, of London, who stands at the head of the Nonconformist bodies of Great Britain, says of the book:—
"It has the charm of personal experience. It is a fascinating story of the successful struggle of a soul towards the light. Moreover, it speaks the truths of the gospel in their simple Bible and New Testament force. It must do much good."

Geo. F. Pentecost, D. D.:—"I have read it with both pleasure and profit. While preserving a spirit of Christian charity and moderation you have succeeded in unmasking the errors of Rome in such a way that the wise as well as the simple may see and understand. I could wish that every Christian minister in the land might not only have a copy of the book, but read it again and again until its trenchant truth would burn like a fire in their bones."

The Rev. Robert Stuart MacArthur, Calvary Baptist Church, New York City, President of the World's Baptist Alliance, says:—
"I have read with special profit and pleasure your book entitled 'The True Faith and How I Found It.' No book of its general character have I ever read with so much advantage. Its narrative is simple and strong. Its expositions of Scripture are scholarly and its spirit is sweet, winsome and thoroughly Christian, and its arguments unanswerable. It will guide all Romanists, whose good fortune it may be to read it, into the light, liberty and love of the gospel of Christ. It is almost as valuable to many Protestants as it is to Romanists.

I wish this book could be circulated by tens of thousands. It is the best campaign document for its purpose with which I am familiar."

Dr. A. B. Leonard, Secretary of the Missionary Society of the Methodist Episcopal Church:—"A timely book. It should be scattered by the hundred thousand among English-speaking Roman Catholics in this country, and it should be translated into German, Spanish and Italian for distribution among those nationalities in America and in their native countries. The book is not controversial, but experimental, and is written in a spirit most commendable. It should be read also by Protestants of all denominations."

William I. Haven, D. D., Secretary American Bible Society:—
"It is one of the most lucid, considerate and convincing statements of the radical difference between Romanism and Protestantism that I have read, and you have written it in such perfect temper that it must win its way to many hearts. It cannot stir up hot feelings because of any ill advised attack upon a historic church."

Bishop J. H. Vincent, D. D.:—"The book is strong and convincing. It is altogether admirable. Its spirit is good. It avoids invective, which it is so difficult to do when a rational mind with a sense of righteousness comes to know just what Rome teaches and just what Rome is. I wish you could scatter the book widely. It ought to be read by Protestants. It is refreshing in these days of apathy to find a book on the market so aggressive, frank and vigorous."

Rev. Ward Platt, D. D.:—"I wish to say of 'The True Faith and How I Found It' that I consider it a classic. It is so convincing a story and so winsome in the telling that all spirit of controversy is banished and one simply drinks in the sweet message and is refreshed. I wish it might be circulated by the hundred thousand and in several languages."

Rev. Dr. Samuel L. Beiler of Boston University:—"It is a fascinating story that would interest thousands if they only knew of it. It would help to hold the Church to its blessed specialty of a conscious salvation that brings peace and joy to the soul and also power to the life."

Rev. Dr. L. D. Watson:—"It is in my judgment the best thing of the kind in print."

Rev. S. A. Morse, D. D., Superintendent of the Olean District writes the author:—"I have fully read your additional chapters and enjoyed every paragraph. It seems to me that the book has a great mission. If it could be circulated by the hundred thousand, Romanism would be much less of a moral and so national threat than it still is. That your book may prove an arsenal to thousands who would otherwise be but poorly armed for the battle is my hope and prayer."

Bishop Joseph F. Berry, D. D.:—"Those new chapters are very strong. The Roman Catholic reader is allured by the fascination of the story in the preceding chapters, and is thus prepared to receive the new part of the work with the clean-cut and conclusive presentation of truth that characterizes the book."

Rev. Dr. L. H. Pearce, in an editorial in his paper, says:— "Your book is unique in most important respects. In temper, scope and strength and in gentleness it is an unusual publication on Romanism. It would be of immense service could it reach the hands of a large number of our Catholic friends."

Price of the book in cloth, 75c. net; paper bound, 35c.

Agents wanted to sell the book in every town or city in America. Liberal commission allowed. Address the Author, 250 W. 25th Street, New York City, or 627 Main Street, Buffalo, N. Y.

Made in the USA